Going South

Unity Hall

Going South

Driving to the South of France

Michael O'Mara Books Limited

To France!

First published in 1992 by
Michael O'Mara Books Limited,
9 Lion Yard, Tremadoc Road, London SW4 7NQ

A CIP catalogue record for this book is available from the
British Library

ISBN 1-85479-150-8

Design and maps: Simon Bell

Typeset by Florencetype Ltd, Kewstoke, Avon
Printed and bound in Great Britain by
Richard Clay Ltd, Bungay, Suffolk

Contents

Foreword

Tragically, my precious wife will never again see her
beloved France. Soon after completing *Going South*, Unity
suffered a stroke of devastating and cruel intensity. She is
paralysed and cannot speak. I am indebted to Unity's god-
daughter, Sue Shephard, and our good friend Dick
Parrack, for all their painstaking work in helping
Catherine Taylor in the final editing.

Philip Wrack
London, 1992

Introduction

It was Dirk Bogarde who first put into my head the idea
of having a home in the hills below Grasse. I had come to
know him while working as a show business reporter on a
national newspaper. In the winter of 1958 the Rank
Organisation had invited me to spend a week with them in
the Dolomites, where they were filming a Hammond
Innes' adventure story, *Campbell's Kingdom*, starring
Bogarde. I had taken a plane to Venice, hired a taxi and
been hurtled, quivering with fear, by a lunatic Italian
driver through blinding snow to Cortina d'Ampezzo, in
the Italian Alps.

Bogarde was on location with his companion, Tony
Forward, and they had arrived in Cortina in a vintage
Rolls-Royce, presumably having driven it from England.
The film's publicity girl, Jean Osborne – a large, efficient
lady with a hefty thirst who happened also to be an extremely good companion – got on well with the rather
difficult Dirk, and everyone got on well with the charming
Tony. I became part of their exclusive little group for the
time I was there.

It was fascinating to be driving around in the splendid
old Rolls, admiring the pink Dolomite mountains. One
crisp morning, as we purred along, Dirk gave what
amounted to a medical lecture on diarrhoea. It seemed a
somewhat unlikely topic for such a screen heart-throb,
whatever the hazards of the local food and water.

But a more interesting observation from Bogarde was
his plaint that England was becoming an impossible place
to live, what with the high taxes and the infuriating

7

schoolgirl fans who besieged his house in Buckinghamshire. He wanted to get out, he said, to live in an old *mas* in the hills below Grasse in the South of France. It was, he assured me, probably the best place in the world to have a home.

I didn't know a *mas* was an old Provençal house, but I did know about the perfume town of Grasse and the thought of living there appealed. On my first trip to the South of France, at the age of 23, I had driven along the Route Napoléon, over the mountains and down to the Mediterranean. The memory of that first glimpse of the impossible blue of the Med, seen from on high behind Grasse, has never faded. In Grasse itself there was a profusion of bougainvillea and other flowers and a seductive, musky scent filled the air. I had thought the town beautiful, but this was my early youth and it was the fleshpots of the coast which beckoned. Grasse was just a place on the way to the beach.

Another journalistic assignment in another country led me nearer to Dirk Bogarde's dream – though by then he was already settled comfortably in his desired old *mas* below the village of Châteauneuf-de-Grasse. It was the time of the French/Algerian war and I went to Morocco to cover a story about the child refugees on the border between Tlemcen in Algeria and Oujda in Morocco. On the way I made friends with a couple in Gibraltar – Hudson, a large, fleshy man with a fine head of white hair and gentle blue eyes, and his wife, Margaret. Hudson was something of a mystery man, involved in some way with secret service activities, and a great companion – well-travelled, trilingual, full of anecdotes and a true gourmet. Hudson lived to eat. Margaret was (and still is) extremely pretty and a touch eccentric. She had long hair which, after one glass of wine too many, she would let down with a theatrical gesture, flinging her thick mane so that it formed circles around her head. Sometimes one had to duck. Though more English than most English, she had never lived in Britain except to go to school.

It was through this couple that I was to find Les Eygages, the small enclave in the hills below Grasse where my husband, Philip, and I now have a home. Hudson and Margaret were fun and we drifted into a friendship which lasted through his postings to Morocco and thence to

Yugoslavia, where I visited them in Belgrade. It was an unwelcoming town, dreary in the extreme, and, though I did not know it, its very dreariness was helping me towards the dream house in France. Hudson and Margaret lived in a charming villa which was permanently rented out to Embassy people, and to mark my arrival in Belgrade there was a cocktail party. To be honest, it was not truly in my honour but had been arranged because Hudson had said I knew the Beatles, which was true, since I was editing a pop magazine called *FAB* at the time. The villa's owner and his wife had a 12-year-old daughter, Dragina. The Beatles had burst through the Iron Curtain, and Dragina was a fan.

We set off for the party, and to my surprise, rapidly followed by horror, went no further than the garage under the house. There, with his wife and daughter, our host waited – a bottle of Slivovitz and tiny glasses at the ready. Hudson's car, a magnificent Ferrari, was in the garage, smelling rather hot as it had not long been parked, and we were to use the elegant bonnet as our table. It was already set out with little saucers of olives and gherkins.

'Why are we down here?' I whispered to Margaret.

'Because they live here,' she whispered back.

I couldn't believe it. A man, a woman and a child shared the garage and a tiny room off it with Hudson's precious Ferrari as the fourth occupant, while the lucky people from the West lived in their house above. It was appalling, though admittedly our hosts did not seem unhappy as we all got rather drunk on plum brandy, repeatedly toasting each other and the Beatles.

But it was no way to live and Margaret said she would not tolerate another winter in Belgrade worrying about the inhabitants of the garage. Hudson capitulated, took early retirement, and he and Margaret left. Which was another step on the road to Les Eygages for me and for them.

One of their great friends was a woman called Joanna Richards, née Miller. She knew brief fame as the author of *One Girl's War*, a book which came out when the Government were having problems with the *Spycatcher* book. Joanna had been in MI5 during the war and had been instrumental in catching a spy. Her book was promptly banned and sold only in Ireland. It was altogether a sad saga, since the book was also published posthumously. She died in Malta in the late '80s. But in the 1960s Joanna was alive and well, spending most of the summer at Les Eygages, and she found a small apartment for Hudson and Margaret in the enclave across from her own house. She was a flamboyant woman, large and generally encased in a defiantly brilliant kaftan. She was generous to a fault and consequently frequently broke. During her broke periods she would let the French house and in the summer of 1960, on Margaret and Hudson's recommendation, she rented it to me.

Six of us went down for a fortnight and found ourselves in a lovely old house with a 40-foot-long terrace overlooking a swimming pool and beyond to extensive if somewhat unkempt grounds. There was a master bedroom with a view over the terracotta roof of the terrace and an *ensuite* bathroom. Downstairs were two more bedrooms looking across the valley to Grasse. These were served by a shower room. There was a spacious living room with lovely views and a big kitchen with an open fireplace. It was shabby but charming, and I fell in love with it the moment we arrived.

It was the air of seclusion and almost secrecy about Les Eygages that appealed. The entrance to the enclave is a huge wooden gate set with a postern. As one enters, there are three tall 17th-century stone houses to the left, standing square on a paved courtyard and facing an olive grove. Further along the courtyard on the right is the landlord's house, which adjoins the one that we had rented. Once upon a time the courtyard had been a village street. The landlord's house and Joanna's portion had been a farm. Underneath this building is the original mill where to this day there are ancient olive-presses and the tall terracotta Ali-Baba jars that held the oil, now all worth a fortune. One of the houses across the courtyard had been the post office, and another housed the butcher. But eventually a new road was built around the property and the owner of Les Eygages erected the wooden gate entrance to the courtyard.

Hudson and Margaret settled in the little apartment right by the wooden gates – the house that was once the post office. It had just two good rooms, with a fair-sized kitchen and bathroom, and it suited Hudson and Margaret perfectly while they looked for a permanent home. Once they had found themselves an apartment in Antibes they offered me what we called the cottage. The landlord, Jean, agreed. As long as I would buy the fixtures and fittings and guarantee the rent, there was no problem.

I took it like a shot. That was 22 years ago. And seven years ago, when Jean asked if Philip and I would like what we still think of as Joanna's house, we took that like a shot, too. At least it was an easy move, though shifting the furniture the length of the courtyard caused Philip to lose half a stone. Unfortunately, the loss was only temporary.

I was hooked on Les Eygages from that very first summer. I loved the lemon and orange trees growing wild in the garden. Brutally big cactus line the paths, cherry trees, greengages and plum trees spill their fruit carelessly. A vine runs the length of the front of the stone houses. I was to find that later in the year there was always a profusion of plums, cherries, greengages, figs and persimmons which no one ever seemed to harvest, for, just seven years later, Les Eygages was to become home. Today Philip and I live for four months of the year in this house, and it is there that I do most of my writing.

In the 22 years since Hudson and Margaret introduced me to Les Eygages I have driven South at least three times a year. Today we make the journey something like four or five times a year, which is wonderful – the only snag being that you have to reach retirement age to have such freedom. But going South is part of my life, and half of the pleasure is in the journey itself.

Over the years I have always tried to set off at slightly different times or from different places so as to arrive somewhere new for the night. Sometimes we use the autoroutes all the way; other times hardly at all. Mostly it's a mixture of the two. We have taken as long as five days to get there and as little as a day and a bit. Never have I done it in one. Why arrive jaded and exhausted? Or, taking into account the way the French drive, possibly not arrive at all.

This book is about the fun I have had and the knowledge I have acquired travelling through France, and I hope both armchair and serious travellers will enjoy it. It is written basically for those who are holidaying in Provence, between Marseilles and Italy, and wishing to get there reasonably quickly. Therefore most of the information is based around the autoroutes. We have assumed that those who may find it useful will not have much time to linger, but hope that our own experiences will make your journey a part of the holiday and not just the chore of getting there.

By the way, I was a very near neighbour of Dirk Bogarde during the long period he was living in France. His Provençal *mas* was about two miles from Les Eygages and we often bumped into each other in the supermarket in the village, both of us wheeling our trolleys.

I was never able to tell him how I had taken his advice to heart. He never recognised me. Or if he did, he wasn't letting on.

Note

Prices are quoted in pounds sterling and are approximate. Distances are measured in kilometres.

The publishers have made every effort to ensure that the information in this book is accurate but would be grateful for any corrections from readers.

1

Your Place is in the Gutter

Driving in France

The first time I drove in France, I wasn't sure I could do it. Driving on the 'wrong' side of the road, in a British Mini, was a scaring prospect. But if I was to enjoy Les Eygages I was going to *have* to drive on French roads.

Quite quickly I became a contented driver in France, whizzing up and down the autoroutes, often on my own, three or four times a year. My secret was that I always drove my own familiar car and told myself firmly that in France I was a guest. And my place was in the gutter! It was the gutter, or the hedge or the ditch, that had to be at my side in a right-hand drive car. Later, when Philip started driving in France, it also worked for him.

Most of the time, driving in France is simple. The times to watch out are on a lonely road without traffic ahead. Then it is all too easy to veer to the wrong side. It is also easy to turn to the wrong side coming out of a turning or going on to (or out of) a roundabout. These are the occasions when paying attention to what you are doing is particularly essential. People grumble that making sure you are in the right lane is difficult, which is true. But getting into the right lane anywhere unfamiliar is always a problem and not one confined to France, though the

13

French are not always as courteous as they might be in
letting foreigners change their minds.

When I was motoring alone I found it much simpler to
drive the autoroutes. Then I had no problems overtaking.
On an ordinary road I might be stuck for miles behind a
lorry or piece of farm machinery because it was impossible
to see what was coming.

As Dickie, our friend and neighbour in Les Eygages,
says, the divorce courts were made for the sort of situation
which can arise so easily on the by-ways of the Continent
in a right-hand drive car. When he first started to drive in
France he would say to Kath, his passenger and wife,
'Anything coming – is it all clear?'

It was a trap question. Kath would answer the first part
of his double question with a 'Yes'. He would assume she
was answering the second part of the question and the
result on more than one occasion was near-disaster. Now
when he wants to overtake, he just asks 'Is it clear?' Kath
gives a simple yes or no.

Having been given the all-clear, it is as well to get on
with it. Driving a right-hand car in France requires a kind
of careful decisiveness or it becomes a question of 'he who
hesitates is lost'. Still, it is fair to say that driving in
France has become much easier for the British over the
years. When I first started driving there the dreaded *priorité à droite* (priority to the right) was in force – which
meant vehicles could and did appear suddenly from a
turning on the right, with every right to do so. There is
still some *priorité à droite* in France, but it is now clearly
signposted, so at least one knows to beware. Also, the
French rules on roundabouts used to be different to ours.
The driver approaching a roundabout had right of way
and, once on, drivers had to keep stopping to give others
access. But in those days France had fewer roundabouts.
In recent years they have gone roundabout mad, and are
building them everywhere. We counted more than 20 in
the area around Les Eygages that were not there two years
ago. They even make double roundabouts.

And they have changed the rules. Now roundabouts
have warning signs: *Vous n'avez pas le priorité* (You don't
have right of way). This is all very well, but elderly
Frenchmen who have been nipping on to roundabouts all
their lives, expecting all to stop before them, are still in-

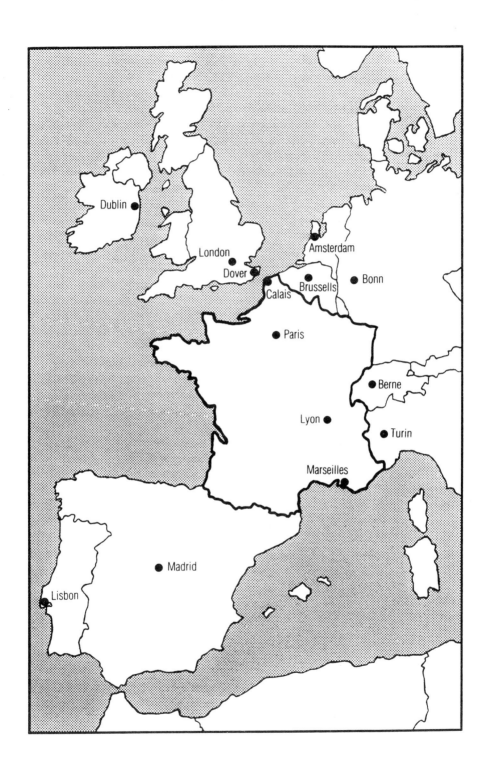

clined to think it is perfectly all right to do so. So at roundabouts it makes sense to proceed with caution.

We did actually witness a brawl between a couple of furious Frenchmen when this new ruling came in. We were relaxing at a pavement café in Avallon, in the Yonne, when the peace was shattered by a great squealing of brakes followed by a blast of car horns. Then came screams of fury from the motorist who had been entering a roundabout, but whose way had been barred by a car already on it – a car which, under the old rules, should have given way. Yells of abuse were not sufficient. The driver of the thwarted car jumped out and ran after his adversary, banging on the car roof with flailing arms as he tried to keep pace with it. I'm afraid we were helpless with laughter.

One particularly dangerous fault the French have is driving in the boot of the car in front. The government are aware of this national failing and are forever launching desperate campaigns to try to persuade drivers to *Gardez votre distance* (Keep your distance) but no-one takes any notice. On the autoroutes they have created test zones of yellow arrows (*marques*) painted in the road. The idea is to accustom French drivers to stay two *marques* behind the next car. One *marque*, they warn, means danger. Two *marques* give security. We watch in baffled amazement as the French manage to crowd two cars into one *marque* while belting along at great speed. It's a waste of yellow paint.

The French also waste an awful lot of money on white paint at zebra crossings. A crossing is there to be parked on (even doubled-parked on) or driven over as fast as possible, regardless of anyone on it. But stop? Never! Out of habit, British drivers do stop for pedestrians, for which the only thanks are hoots from the car behind, plus a suspicious glare from the pedestrian who believes that it is some wicked trick of *perfide Albion* to run him over while his defences are down.

*

Motoring Manners

It is a pity, but the only thing wrong with French roads is French drivers. The French are a courteous nation. They are kind to children and old people and will hold open doors with an engaging smile. To be the recipient of their hospitality can be embarrassing, so generous are they. They are meticulous about saying 'please' and 'thank you' and are probably the most civilised race on earth, but put them behind the wheel of a car and they become raving, competitive lunatics – impatient and often downright dangerous.

We were once driving through the little town of Tournus in Saône-et-Loire (a great stopping place with a wide choice of restaurants and hotels, incidentally) looking for a left-hand turning to go down to have a look at the river Saône. I was studying the map, and therefore we were driving slowly. I accept this can give a French driver an attack of apoplexy but it had an even worse effect on the driver behind us. He became murderous. He began by hooting wildly and followed by driving in our boot until Philip stopped to let him pass, waving him on with, admittedly, an irritated hand. The middle-aged, bullet-headed driver with his wife beside him came half-way past, with perhaps a centimetre to spare, still hooting. He then proceeded first to side-swipe us (luckily just managing to miss) and then, once ahead, jerked his car along the road in front of us, constantly stopping dead and starting again, all the while making rude signs out of the side window.

We were somewhat astounded by this dangerous behaviour. But there were consolations. He obviously had great faith in the skill of a British driver, considering the chances he was taking. And, as Philip said thoughtfully once we had found our turning, 'I bet his wife isn't half giving him hell.'

The best way to survive French drivers is to wave them on and keep your cool.

In turn, the French think that the British lack *politesse* because we do not say 'please' and 'thank you' nearly enough for their taste. It is obligatory to say *Bonjour* or *Bonsoir, messieurs dames* whenever entering a bar or restaurant, and to repeat it when you leave. You must also be sure to begin any conversation in a shop or restaurant with *Bonjour* or *Bonsoir*. A smile is not sufficient. And to forget to say *s'il vous plaît* after any request is considered unforgivable. Philip and I had once waited in a long queue at Nice station to try to find out if it were possible to board a fast train from there to Rome and exactly how long the journey would take. The ebullient, slightly eccentric man behind the information desk dealt with questions with great panache until it was our turn. I smiled at him, I was pleasant as possible, but I did not say *Bonjour* before I asked the question. He proceeded to regale the entire station with information on the rudeness of the British, perhaps not realising that I understood French as well as I do (since I speak it so badly). I fear he made me cross, and as my French is always improved by a soupçon of indignation, I told him so and it was his turn to apologise. But he had a point. I had forgotten the sacred *Bonjour*. Though I have been a regular traveller in France since the early '50s, it is still possible to make this elementary dent in the preservation of the *entente cordiale*.

Pick a Road

The first time I was driven to the South of France was in 1952 and there was only one tiny length of autoroute, in the South, outside Valence. One drove through the middle of Paris, or veered to the East and went through Reims. There were complicated ways of avoiding Paris, but on the whole it was just as quick to drive through the capital. Lyons was always a solid jam and it seemed impossible not to get lost there. And yet the journey never took all that long. There was little traffic out of the towns and one could buzz along the N6 and N7 hardly seeing another car. We used to reckon on about 10 hours' driving after Paris.

Those days are gone. But driving in France is still pleasant, though in an entirely different way. The country is amazingly well served for roads and there are usually several different ways of getting anywhere, depending on your mood and the time available. Roughly speaking, there are three types of routes one can take. Of these, the most pleasant to drive if you are not in a hurry are the **D roads**. These are usually extraordinarily deserted and in first-class condition. D roads, usually marked in yellow on a Michelin map, though the more superior of them are sometimes marked in red, are often good short cuts, well worth taking if the traffic is heavy on the Routes Nationales – the **N roads**, always marked in red on your Michelin. Before the motorways these were the main routes and are still well maintained and frequently improved. We prefer, however, to take a D road rather than an N route. Many of the N routes still suffer heavy traffic and are often three lanes – tricky for visibility when driving a British car. The third class of roads, the **autoroutes**, are excellent but expensive. If you drove the autoroute from Calais to Nice, it would set you back about £35 in tolls. Remember, when planning your holiday, that this cost doubles if you come back the same way. But it is possible to get some use out of the autoroutes without paying – or by paying very little – though you will notice that because the section is toll-free it is busy.

The autoroutes are inexpensive or free from:
Calais to St Omer, £1 (join it from the boat)
Both sides of Paris, from Roissy-en-France to Fleury (join it from the **N17** going South, from the **N7** going North) and from Pontoise and Mantes to the Périphérique, coming from Le Havre, Dieppe or Caen
Around Reims from Reims-la-Neuvillettes to Cormontreuil (join it from the **N44**)
Around Lyon from Limonest to the other side of Vienne (join it from the **N6** going South, **N7** going North)
Around Aix-en-Provence from Salon de Provence to Lançon (just a few francs; join it from the **N7** going South)
To Cannes from Puget-s-Argens. Then only a few francs until the other side of Nice (join it from the **N8**)
From Le Havre to the Pont de Tankerville
From St Etienne to Vienne (join it from the **N82**)

These free or nearly free stretches are well worth taking, as they do by-pass towns where there are usually serious hold-ups. It is, for example, total madness *not* to take the autoroute around Lyon. Before the autoroute was built through this town it was always a major blackspot. It could take up to three hours to get across. It is still crowded even with the autoroute and can take a long time, particularly when the impatient French crash into each other – not usually seriously, but enough to cause a lot of shouting, bawling and waving of arms as well as hooting from those held up. Today you are unlikely to get lost in Lyon if you stick to the autoroute. However, it is as well not to arrive there around mid-day, when the hungry populace are trying to rush home for lunch, or around 2.30pm, when they are trying to rush back to work. The autoroute through the town becomes a crawling mass of traffic. Best to stop off for lunch yourself in this instance, though normally the very best time to drive in France is at lunchtime, from about 12.30pm, when the roads become mysteriously deserted and a lot of progress can be made.

High Days and Holidays

It is always best to take into account French national holidays when you plan to drive through France. If you wish to sample hell on earth try driving South on either the first or last weekends of July or August. Driving North at those times is not much better, particularly at the end of August. Every inhabitant of northern Europe appears to be on the move during those weekends, and don't kid yourself that you might escape the worst of it by driving at night. Night driving, with everyone tearing down from Paris in the dark, can, unless you have nerves of steel, leave you a gibbering wreck. If you are driving South in July and August, pick the middle weeks of the month.

There is a list of French national holidays at the back of the book. Watch out particularly for *Toussaint*, All Saints' Day. It falls on November 1st and is followed the next day by All Souls' Day, 'the day of the dead'. *Toussaint* is a national holiday that generally falls in the middle of the week and the French, like the British, are apt to turn the day into a long weekend, if not a week. They call this

extension of holiday 'the bridge.' It is also on this first
weekend in November that every camping-mad German
and Dutchman takes the caravan or trailer home ready for
winter. Or there are others, like us, who have packed up
their summer homes until next spring. The autoroute is
busy. For *Toussaint* and All Souls' every florist shop,
supermarket, market stall and *pépinière* (garden nursery)
has countless pots of chrysanthemums on sale. At this
time, families visit their dead, and every little cemetery is
a mass of chrysanthemums in all colours and sizes. This
has, I might add, put me off chrysanthemums for life.

There is much the same performance on May Day (May
1st), the *Fête du Travail*. Again florists, market stalls, etc,
are open but this time to sell little pots of lilies of the
valley, which neighbours and friends present to each
other. Lilies of the valley are the symbol for May Day and
significant in a Roman Catholic country because they are
supposed to have grown from the tears shed by the Virgin
Mary at the Cross.

Generally speaking, May is not a good time to be jour-
neying. The French celebrate May Day on the 1st,
promptly followed by VE day on May 8th, a national
holiday with church parades and tricolours flying everywhere. Hot on the heels of that comes Ascension Day,
which falls 40 days after Easter. Then comes *La Pentecôte*
nearer the end of the month, 50 days after Easter. May
sometimes appears to be one long 'bridge' when driving in
France.

Using the Autoroutes

The autoroutes are not to be feared. Except at high
season and special weekends they are not as crowded as
British roads, and are extremely well signposted and simple to use. As you go through the *péage* you *prenez un
ticket* – take a ticket from a machine which then lifts a
barrier to let you on. Some of the more modern ticket
dispensers even speak. They welcome you with a recorded
announcement and then send you on your way with a
cheerful message of caution. You normally hand over your

ticket at the other end of your journey and pay the man or woman in the booth (not forgetting to say *Bonjour*). If you lose your ticket they will charge you as if you have driven the full length of the autoroute.

Occasionally there will be large signs as you near the *péage* telling you to '*préparez XX francs*' – meaning that you should have ready whatever sum of francs they require. Then you merely throw this amount into a machine which counts the money, sometimes even gives change, (*monnaie*) and opens the barrier to let you through. If you do not have the right change there is one booth for drivers *sans monnaie*.

The only problem is that, not unnaturally, all the booths are to the left of the car. When driving a right-hand car without a passenger to assist this creates difficulties, particularly if the car does not have electric windows. Stretching over to unwind the window and reach for the ticket with a queue behind you can be nerve-wracking. When driving alone I always finished the journey with a strained shoulder. There is no solution to this that I can think of except to take a friend. In Calais there is now one *caisse* (cash point) especially for drivers of right-hand cars. Maybe more will appear.

Stopping places and petrol stations are plentiful on the autoroutes and are signalled well in advance. The stopping places, called *aires*, are excellent, with clean lavatories, picnic areas with rough wooden tables and chairs, often children's playgrounds and usually a telephone. *Aire*, incidentally, does not mean fresh air, but space or area, and indeed *les aires* are very spacious.

As well as shops, autoroute garages usually have at least some kind of snack bar or, at best, a restaurant attached. Either of these are considerably pleasanter than motorway stops in Britain. Neither will serve wine or alcohol unless you are eating but it is legally permitted to have a glass of wine with a meal.

Motorway garages will generally accept credit cards, though some of the Elf service stations (known to us as the National Elf Service) refuse them, except where there are automatic dispensers. With these you must have a credit card or cash to insert into the pump to make it work. I fear we have never mastered this complicated procedure and when I see the word *automatic* under the picture of a petrol pump we head straight for the next garage.

It is very unwise to change money into francs at any service station. They may take as much as 10% for the privilege. Always change your money at a bank.

If you should have the misfortune to break down there are signs every kilometre or so which point in the direction of the nearest bright orange telephone, saving all that toss-up of which direction to trudge in. And don't be surprised if you see a courageous man, dressed in bright orange, flagging down the traffic in the middle of road-works on an autoroute. He is just an extremely convincing robot.

French traffic police can be very tough. If they catch you speeding it's a fine on the spot, and no good bleating that you've run out of francs. The fine can be anything between £150 and £300, depending on the severity of the offence.

The same applies if you are seen driving over an unbroken white line. I once got caught for taking a corner too wide, even though I could see perfectly well that there was no other car coming towards me. Out from behind a tree leapt a policeman. Don't think they'll let you off because you are British: they won't.

Speed limits are 37 mph (60 kph) in built up areas; 56 mph (90 kph) on single-carriageway roads; 68 mph (110 kph) on dual carriageways and 80 mph (130 kph) on motorways.

There are new speed limits in force in France for driving on wet roads. You are supposed to be aware of these even though they are not posted. You should not drive at over 68 mph (110 kph) on wet toll roads; 49 mph (80 kph) on others.

Finding your Way

There is absolutely no doubt (in my mind, anyway) that the best maps to use in France are Michelin – and not just the large one (Number 989) that covers the whole of France, though this is necessary to plot your journey as a whole. Having established which way you wish to go it is best to make sure you have handy the area maps covering each section of your journey, plus the Guide Michelin itself. The area maps complement the guide. If you see a town underlined in red, you will find it mentioned in the guide as having either recommended hotels or restaurants.

The maps are meticulous, with distances marked even on the smallest roads. They are very simple to use and astonishingly informative, with references to churches, ruins and even large factories, all of which help to make the journey easier. The maps are corrected every year and also dated, which means that you always know if you are using an up-to-date one. You will find the year of production printed in the top left-hand corner of the map. Always check the date before you buy to make sure you are not buying old stock.

Michelin maps also sketch in planned autoroutes as well as those under construction. These are indicated by broken yellow and red lines which become more positive as the road nears completion. Often the date of the road's opening will be shown. It will read in red *fin 1991* or *prévu fin 19 . . ..*

France is extremely well signposted. Cross a bridge over a river and there is a sign giving you even the tiniest river's name. Philip's theory is that in Britain we took down the signposts during the last war and have never properly got round to putting them back. In France they signpost everything. Entering a village in the South you are greeted by a signpost listing every shop and amenity; streets even have signposts listing all the house names. Every few miles on the roads you come across a good, solid stone milestone which has the number of the route clearly painted at the top. The route number also is sited separately on top of signposts at every turning. Since your map also marks road numbers it is simple to check that you are in the right place.

There are so many aids for the traveller. For example, if you find yourself in Paris looking for an address, bear in mind that the street numbers are almost always printed on the lamp-post opposite the property. Why can't we do that?

In towns, it is obviously necessary to be aware of which next major town you are heading for, but if you don't see it mentioned on the first signpost you come to, do not panic. Follow *toutes directions* or *autres directions* until you do. *Toutes directions* (all directions) and *autres directions* (other directions) usually create a sort of ring road around the town, eventually leading you to the turning you need and steering you away from the town centre. You can also avoid congested centres by following the *poids lourds* signs which are routes to take heavy lorries away from the middle of the town.

You will also come across some rather curious and sometimes alarming road signs that the French put out as warnings, sometimes merely scrawled on boards: warnings such as *risque d'inondation* (risk of flooding) or *chaussée déformée* – meaning that the road surface is uneven. These individualistic signs can offer information about *betterave* (beetroot) or *boue* (mud) on the road. You will find a list of these mysterious warnings and the more common ones, in alphabetical order, at the back of this book.

Distances are marked in kilometres, and as you will be travelling in kilometres we have used them throughout the book. If you prefer to think in miles, the simple sum to convert kilometres is to divide by eight and multiply by five. I usually carry a calculator so that I can do the sum quickly. It also gives me something to do while Philip drives. It is useful to have some occupation for the passenger as there are some parts of the journey where the scenery is not spectacular enough to keep awake and it always feels so mean to collapse into slumber while someone else is driving.

Riffling through the Michelin guide for the night's stopping place is a useful way of passing the time. If you are on the autoroute it is comparatively easy to work out where you will be at a given time. If you are driving at 75 mph and intend to drive for two more hours the chances are you will need to look for a spot 240 kilometres away unless something goes wrong.

I also pass the time by spotting where other cars have come from. The French licensing system is different from the British. A car must be registered in the *département* in which its owner lives and the *département* number is the last two figures of the number-plate. If the owner moves to another *département* he must re-register his car and is given a new number plate. For the benefit of all fidgety passengers you will find a list of the *département* numbers

25

at the back of this book so that you can match the car with
its origin.

Eating and Sleeping

Remember that the Michelin guide is not the only auth-
ority on hotels and restaurants. There are guides for both
the Logis and Relais de France – always excellent hotels
and restaurants, though most of these find themselves in
the Michelin pages. There are guides to Routier eating –
roadside restaurants frequented by long-distance lorry
drivers and always excellent value. The AA and the RAC
will provide you with special routes – at a price – and they
also produce guides. My own favourite is Michelin, for
which the hotels and restaurants are inspected unknow-
ingly until, to their delight, they are told that their name
is to appear in this bible of guides. As an added protection
for impartiality, should a hotel be unwise enough to adver-
tise the fact that it is mentioned by Michelin, it is immediately struck off the list.

It is worth sitting down with the Michelin and studying
it before you set off on your journey. Enjoy the fun of
deciding where you might stay. It won't describe a restaurant for you but it will tell you what it costs and give
you an idea of its standards. It won't tell you much about
the décor of an hotel or warn if it's opposite the town's
marshalling yards, but it will tell you whether or not you
are expected to eat in its restaurant if you stay there, or let
you know if the hotel doesn't have a restaurant, as well as
a mass of other detail. Learn to use the guide before you
set off on your travels. Use your guide to check that the
hotel you have in mind is not closed for *its* annual holiday.

The frequent question on the subject of travelling
through France is: Do you or don't you book accommodation? We never do, making our decisions about a bed
for the night at the time we are ready to stop. We dislike
being bound to stop at some place we may not fancy when
we reach it, having left behind hotels which looked irresistible. It's fun to be free. But then we never drive much
after six o'clock out of season or five o'clock in season –

even earlier, if we are mad enough to be on the road
during the first or last weekends of July and August.

If you don't reserve a room, you must stop in good time
and if you want to keep driving until late, then you should
reserve and, if possible, pay in advance. If it gets late, and
the room is not paid for, the French (great believers in a
bird in the hand) are quite likely to give your reserved
room to someone else. Once, at 1am, I came off the boat
from Dover to Boulogne which had been delayed by fog. I
was not alarmed, since I had already reserved my room at
the *Hôtel Metropole*, chosen because it happened to be the
nicest hotel in Boulogne. It was the first time I had ever
bothered with such a precaution.

However, my confidence was misplaced. On arrival the
place was bolted and barred with not a light to be seen. I
shouted, banged, hollered and eventually a sleepy member
of staff opened the door. The hotel was full; they had
given away my room, even knowing that I would be arriving late from England on a dark and foggy night. This was
another occasion when fury salted my grasp of the French
language, but it didn't get me a room at the inn. I have
never, on principle, stayed at that hotel again. This is
probably cutting off my nose to spite my face, but I don't
care. And I have never bothered to book since.

If you have set your heart on staying somewhere truly
luxurious like a converted château or a hotel with three
stars for food, or a grand hotel in one of the bigger towns,
then it does make sense to make a reservation, particularly
at weekends. If you are looking for somewhere simple,
this is less of a necessity. And if all else should fail, the
local *Palais des Sports* (one of those big cafés with the
billiards table, football games and pinball machines so
beloved by the French) often have simple accommodation
if you enquire. The room will be spotlessly clean and will
amaze you with its cheapness.

Wherever you decide to stay, the procedures are rather
different from those in Britain. For one thing, by law, the
French must display a menu outside their establishment,
so you can see before you enter whether you fancy what is
on offer and, more importantly, how much the meal is
going to cost. Check to see if it says *taxes et service compris*;
it means that a tip is included in the price, though if the
service has been exceptional, you may want to leave a few

francs extra. There will generally be at least three set
menus from which to choose. One, the tourist menu, will
be inexpensive and simple. The second will offer a larger
choice and the third is usually the *gastronomique*.

Most restaurants do have an *à la carte*, but it is best to
stick to a set menu. It's possible that if you order *à la
carte*, choosing dishes that are on different menus, the bill
can come to more than one of the menus would have cost
in the first place.

No-one will be surprised if you ask to see the room
(*chambre*) that the hotel is offering. In fact, they may automatically take you to see the accommodation. If you don't
like the room, ask to see another. It is a legal requirement
in France to display the price of the room and the breakfast. Nine times out of 10 you find it printed on a card
behind the bedroom door, but if not there, try the back of
the bathroom door. Also, the French are big on family
rooms, particularly in simple hotels. They always have
rooms which will take up to four bodies. Of course, these
are meant for parents and children, but if four of you are
travelling together, and you want to economise, no-one
will look askance if you ask for a family room (*chambre
famille*).

Compared with Britain, the price of hotel rooms in
France is astonishingly inexpensive and always good value.
Some years ago I found myself stuck in Compiègne in
Northern France, having driven far too late. It was nearly
11pm and every hotel was full. In desperation I asked at a
Café des Sports and was given a small, clean room with a
wash-basin and bidet. At first they said no, but I must
have looked so dismayed that the proprietress relented. It
was perfectly adequate. The loo was down the hall but at
£4 for the night I wasn't going to grumble about that. I
left this vast sum on the hall table as I let myself out the
next morning, making sure the door was locked behind
me. I could have left without paying and taken the clock
with me for all the interest anyone took in my departure.
The old-fashioned French do have a touching faith in the
honesty of the British.

There are those who scorn the thought of wasting
money on overnight accommodation and make the drive
to the South in one day. Or, even more insanely, one
night. It is perfectly possible, particularly if there are two

drivers in the car, but a headlong dash through France is unwise and takes away a lot of the pleasure that the changing scenery of the country has to offer. To roll gently from the grey prim villas and the opaline colours of the North to the red roofs and blaze of yellows of the South adds to the appreciation of the holiday. There is more to France than Provence, so try to stop for one night *en route* if you possibly can, making the stop a positive part of the holiday.

Even more importantly, if you take your time, you are much more likely not only to travel hopefully but to arrive safely.

And don't forget: when you first get back to Britain, keep to the left!

2

Autumn Journey

A Trip South and Back

It was late Autumn when we made our fifth trip of the
year to Les Eygages. We had left friends there when we
returned to England in mid-September and not having a
femme de ménage needed to go back to shut up shop for the
winter. It is not that we are too mean to employ a cleaner.
The problem is finding one. The South of France is a
wealthy area and not too many women want to be polish-
ing someone else's home. One solution is to employ a
woman through an agency but the agencies usually don't
want to know unless they are also letting the property, and
we don't let.

Come the winter, the house does lose some of its charm
for us. The slow rise of land up to the Alpes Maritimes
behind the Côte D'Azur may be wonderfully hot and som-
nulent in the summer but in them thar Alpine foothills the
winters can become quite nasty and chilly. Our old house,
with its 4-foot-thick walls, holds both the cold and the
heat with equal ease. Once it gets cold inside, it stays
cold. The problem is exacerbated by the fact that French
electricity is decidedly quirky and since we have electric
central heating, warmth and comfort are not automatic.
Turn on a couple of radiators and put on the electric
kettle for a quick cuppa and out goes the lot. We know
why electric kettles are rarely on sale in France. Even
turning on one extra light can deliver the *coup de grâce*.
This explains why our house has as many torches as a

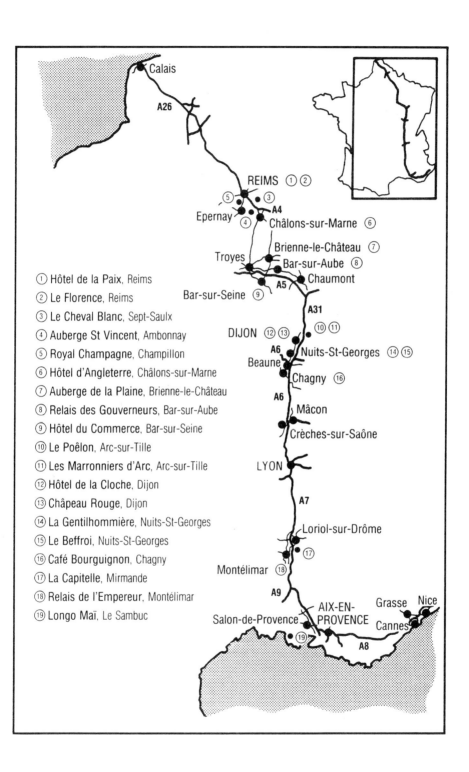

Calais

A26

REIMS ① ②

⑤ ● ③

Epernay ④ ● A4
Châlons-sur-Marne ⑥

Brienne-le-Château ⑦
Troyes
Bar-sur-Aube ⑧

① Hôtel de la Paix, Reims
A5
Chaumont

② Le Florence, Reims
Bar-sur-Seine ⑨

③ Le Cheval Blanc, Sept-Saulx
A31

④ Auberge St Vincent, Ambonnay
DIJON ⑫ ⑬
⑩ ⑪

⑤ Royal Champagne, Champillon
A6
Nuits-St-Georges ⑭ ⑮

Beaune

⑥ Hôtel d'Angleterre, Châlons-sur-Marne
Chagny ⑯

⑦ Auberge de la Plaine, Brienne-le-Château
A6

⑧ Relais des Gouverneurs, Bar-sur-Aube
Mâcon

⑨ Hôtel du Commerce, Bar-sur-Seine
Crèches-sur-Saône

⑩ Le Poêlon, Arc-sur-Tille

⑪ Les Marronniers d'Arc, Arc-sur-Tille
LYON

⑫ Hôtel de la Cloche, Dijon

⑬ Châpeau Rouge, Dijon
A7

⑭ La Gentilhommière, Nuits-St-Georges

⑮ Le Beffroi, Nuits-St-Georges
Loriol-sur-Drôme

⑯ Café Bourguignon, Chagny
⑰

⑰ La Capitelle, Mirmande
Montélimar ⑱

⑱ Relais de l'Empereur, Montélimar
A9
Grasse Nice

⑲ Longo Maï, Le Sambuc
AIX-EN-
PROVENCE
Salon-de-Provence
Cannes
⑲
A8

convention of cinema usherettes and why we stay in London from late November until March.

Normally the problem in the hills is not intense cold but damp. And, of course, damp can cause more damage to a house than cold. So come the autumn we make this special journey (which is also a marvellous excuse) to put the house into hibernation.

When we set off to perform our autumnal chore on this occasion, I had just sold a new book and the advance was due, so we decided to be a little self-indulgent. We would make our overnight stops at hotels the Michelin guide had awarded with a little black château sign. Not, alas, a double red château sign – the advance hadn't been that big!

Continuing our policy of always setting off at slightly different times so that we land up each evening at somewhere new, Philip had booked the P & O noon ferry from **Dover to Calais**. We always go by P & O, as Philip has the regulation £600 worth of shares, which allow us concessionary half-price fares on P & O ferries – a serious consideration when you cross the channel with your car as often as we do. Those shares have paid for themselves time and time again. (Incidentally, if you have £300 worth the reduction on fares is 25%.)

He had also booked into the club class cabin as a hedge against hordes of schoolchildren running amok and the lager louts who are only there for the beer. This club class crossing does not yet seem to have caught on, probably because P & O don't make a fuss about it in their literature. We were chatting to a policeman and his French wife and they said they had stopped crossing the Channel by ferry because they could not stand the drunken rabble. No doubt he spent the journey restraining the reflex to make an arrest. But for £10 extra a head the super-ferries provide accommodation in a large, private, well-furnished lounge with its own bar and loos. You get free coffee and biscuits, the day's newspapers and a ship-to-shore telephone plus waiter service for drinks and sandwiches.

We were somewhat dismayed to find ourselves on an unfamiliar ferry – the *Pride of Bruges* – which was small and a little shabby after the super-ferries on which we try to travel. The ship was almost deserted and we were chagrined to discover that a public lounge, set with small tables and chairs outside the restaurant, looked considerably more comfortable and prettier than the club lounge where the seats were lined up in rows, all facing to the front. All that was missing was the cinemascope screen. And the loos were one deck down. This was a sharp lesson to check which ferry is running before chucking away a tenner on club class. But *Pride of Bruges* did have some advantages. It was one of our fastest crossings ever, taking one hour and 12 minutes. We wondered if they were practising for the opening of the Channel Tunnel, and the added competition which that would bring.

The weather forecast had not been good. We were supposed to have strongish winds, moderate seas and some rain. As it happened the crossing was a cliché of a mill-pond and the sun shone all the way. We were off and on the road South nearly half-an-hour earlier than we had expected. The helpful *douane* let everyone through without hold-up (anxious to be off for their lunch, no doubt) and we set off on what we grandly consider to be our own private autoroute – the **A26** from Calais to Reims. For this journey we had picked one of those brief periods when the time in France is the same as in Britain. France is usually one hour ahead of the UK throughout the year but they change their clocks for nearly a month from the end of September. This makes a useful difference to the drive as normally one immediately loses an hour arriving in France. It is regained on the way home, of course, but somehow time doesn't seem so important on the journey back.

We set off in bright sunshine on the **A26**. This is a most extraordinary autoroute, and one that we recommend – even if rather reluctantly, as we would just as soon it didn't get too popular. It doesn't seem to matter which time of the day, day of the week or week of the year we go, the almost new surface is guaranteed to be practically deserted. The road sweeps on majestically through the gentle countryside of the Pas-de-Calais, uncovering a vista of small villages pin-pointed by lead-pencil church spires, with endless fields devoted to agriculture. On Sundays, travellers see men striding out with dog and gun, shooting for their supper. At one point on the road there is always the mysterious smell of onions, without an onion-field or pickling factory to be seen. Here and there in the distance are the great slagheaps from abandoned coal-mines, now growing green like Roman burial mounds, and the heart-tearing, real war burial grounds of small white crosses which spatter the Northern French landscape.

The Pas-de-Calais and Picardy have no spectacular scenery. All they have to offer is undemanding, soft country-side in opaline colours to rest the eyes and soothe the soul. Above all, this part of France is peaceful. It is only those white crosses and the many memorials to the fallen, jutting bravely into the sky, that give a reminder of two bloody world wars which were fought on this gentle soil.

If you were going South entirely by motorway, you would leave the **A26** and take the **A1** where the two motorways link and breeze on until you eventually arrive at the Périphérique – a highly effective, though busy, ring road which the French ruthlessly carved around their capital. (More of the Paris route to the South later.) If you *do* go through Paris you can drive from Calais to Naples without seeing a traffic light. Come to that, you can drive to Copenhagen from Naples without seeing a traffic light, but for the moment, let us stay on the **A26**, where the road sweeps round well to the East of Paris, avoiding the city completely.

Today, on this Eastern route, there is only one more stretch of motorway to be built – the 80-odd km between Châlons-sur-Marne and Troyes. Once this is complete it will also be possible to get to the deep South and back on this route without seeing a traffic light. Work has started, and it is possible that the last stretch will be opened by the late summer of 1992. Do check with the AA or the RAC if you are setting off about this time to see if work is completed. We suspect that eventually the road will become more popular than the A1, cutting out as it does the Périphérique. This route is actually shorter than going via Paris, and even using the remaining ordinary road on the route we follow, we find it a much pleasanter drive.

It was some years ago when we began taking the incomplete Eastern route to the south. We started at the time when the French opened the last stage of the Southbound **A26** to Reims in the late '80s. For our purposes they were a bit late with it. I had been writing a book which was set in Champagne and we made numerous journeys to Reims for some extremely pleasant research.

Before the **A26** was completed, the road from St
Quentin through to Reims was a mixture of the dangerous
three lanes, some dual carriageway and some single. We
were more or less forced to go that way on research trips,
but when going South we decided to go through Paris.
This meant suffering the traffic jams and the tension of
the Périphérique. If you hit Paris at the wrong time the
Périphérique can add as much as a couple of hours to the
journey and the standard of driving is so bad at rush hour
that you can come off it a jaded wreck.

It was good news when the Reims autoroute was completed. It by-passes the whole of the Champagne city –
while giving dramatic views of the stately bulk of the
Cathedral – and then, renamed the **A4**, whizzes on to
Châlons-sur-Marne, 45km down the road. There it runs
out.

Going South, from Châlons-sur-Marne (not to be con-
fused with Chalon-sur-Saône) after the end of the **A4** it is
back to ordinary roads before picking up a different autoroute beyond the town of Troyes. This will no longer be
necessary once the final stretch is completed.

But as long as the road is not too busy, Philip finds an
N or a D highway a rest from endless motorway and we
worked out a route which manages to miss almost all traffic. (More private roads!) Also, it is disappointing, not to
say monotonous, to drive through France without ever
going through a village or seeing any form of human life
that is not encased in a motor car. Even now that the
autoroute has been extended we will probably still drive
this peaceful road, simply because we enjoy it.

On this particular trip we had just about arrived at
Reims (280km and three hours at the most from Calais
taking it reasonably easy) when the weather lived up to the
forecast. It began to rain. By the time we reached
Châlons-sur-Marne we were experiencing one of those
downpours when the water runs straight up the windows
and sounds as if someone is beating dozens of tiny ham-
mers on the car roof. Visibility was awful.

We had planned to stay the night at Vitry-le-François
since the beautiful Olga, one of our neighbours at Les
Eygages, comes from this nice little Northern French
town, but it was another 32km away. It was getting on for
4pm and the strength of the rain was causing us to crawl.

Châlons-
sur-Marne

A rapid vote settled for a stay at or near **Châlons-sur-Marne**.

We have found when travelling through France that if the weather is good and the evenings not too short, it is more pleasant to stay in either a small town or deep in the country. If it is pouring with rain, or getting dark, we prefer to head for brighter lights. The French in the provinces have an entirely different pattern of living to us. They are mostly out-of-bed and out-of-doors much earlier than we are, but they batten down the shutters and retire to bed as early as 9.30pm. This does not make for much of a night-life in the country. Some villages you would think are shut. Permanently.

The Michelin gives prices and they are rarely out of date, providing you have the current year's edition. Using its pages, we decided to chance a small town, L'Epine, where there was an hotel, *Aux Armes de Champagne*, which the Michelin were pretty complimentary about in their own abrupt way. It would cost around £50 for a room and was 7km outside Châlons-sur-Marne. It was one of those awkward places to get to, involving travelling round in circles and driving under main roads, but since it was well signposted we got there.

It looked charming. An old-world, half-timbered building near a spectacular basilica far too big for the village. Leaving Philip badly parked while I dashed through the rain to see if they had a room, I was greeted by one of those *chic*, faintly masculine-looking Northern French women who said with unconcealed glee: '*Complet! Complet! Complet!*' while throwing in a dismissive gesture and a triumphant smile to make her point that they were Full! Full! Full!

Had we been further South, the lady would have been desolate that she could not accommodate us. She would have suggested another hotel, and we would have left believing that she sincerely regretted that her establishment would not have the pleasure of our company.

Years of travelling in France have proved indisputably the difference between the North and the South. I recall travelling North many years ago with my friend Joanna Richards. She had been living in the South for five months and had become accustomed to the Southern way of doing things. We managed to lose ourselves in Arras, which is

just a short step from Belgium. Eventually we found a
pedestrian who willingly gave us directions with great
courtesy and precision. Joanna launched into a Southern
tirade of extravagant gratitude. She thanked him a million
times, she told him how amazingly *gentil* he was, ending
up by saying, '*Merci, merci, merci bien.*'

The man looked at her with eyes narrowed by deep
suspicion, decided she had to be taking the mickey, and
snarled something very rude indeed, which basically
suggested what she and I could do to ourselves. The sort
of remark, indeed, I was tempted to make to the
receptionist at the *Armes de Champagne*.

However, I admitted defeat politely and we drove back
into Châlons-sur-Marne where in the Guide the *Hôtel
d'Angleterre* enjoyed the same general recommendation as
Aux Armes de Champagne, boasting a star for food. After a
lifetime of avoiding hotels called 'England,' we decided to
try it. It turned out to be a nice old building on the corner
of the Place Mgr Tissier and Rue Carnot. Another boyish
girl, but this one with a round, cheerful face and smile,
said, Yes, they had a room, and wanted to know if we
wanted a double bed, a bath, a shower, dinner?

We were delighted that the *Aux Armes de Champagne*
was *complet*. The *Angleterre* must be one of the nicest
medium-priced hotels in France. The room was not enormous, but had big twin beds, pushed together and
covered with one large and elegant bedcover. Philip, who
had asked for single beds in case he was restless, remarked
that we had the best of both worlds. There was a large
wardrobe and a long dressing table, both modern, a mini-
bar, a television and one huge black-mirrored wall. Hotel
design is not always a strong point in France, but here
they had got it right in a modern kind of way. Particularly
the bathroom, which was a dream in grey marble with a
spacious bath *and* a separate glassed-in shower, separate
loo and all the works – shower caps, soap in a nice little
box, shampoo and bubble bath. It seemed to us like a
smaller version of that expensive stronghold of the
Kennedy family – the Carlyle Hotel in New York. The
only difference was that where a room in the Carlyle sets
you back about £250 a night, this was about £50.

Our room had a charming view over the little church of
Notre-Dame-en-Vaux and the life of what appeared to be

a prosperous little town. It was too miserable to eat or drink on their flowery terrace, guarded by two fine stone lions, so we sat in the smart bar in big black leather seats. The terrace must look lovely in summer, set out with white wrought-iron furniture and shaded by a big feathery tree, but rain stopped play. We took our excellent dinner in the busy, well-run restaurant, appointed to the same standard of décor as the bedrooms. The theme colour was warm coral, with peachy table linen, and since the restaurant was large, the acres of space had been broken with white trellis-work screens and potted palms. The restaurant, owned by Jacky Michel, makes a speciality of game and fish and, not surprisingly, they have *une grande sélection* of champagne. As we were still *just* in Champagne we started with a couple of glasses. They brought us plates of tiny *bonne bouches* (good mouthfuls) of delicious but mysterious fish dishes to begin and truffles and extravagant *petits fours* at the end of the meal with the coffee. A half-bottle of good wine each was included in the menu price. This was certainly not excessive, as the most expensive menu was £40; the cheapest £20.

Breakfast was a knockout. Freshly squeezed orange juice, a pot of yoghurt, a big jug of coffee *each*, plenty of butter, two big pots of different *confiture* and the usual breads and croissants. With somewhere to lock up the car and a morning paper on the breakfast table, the bill for the night was just over £100.

The *Angleterre*, though not cheap, is an excellently run hotel. It is really rather smart. There's nothing old-world about it, but for those looking for real comfort and cossetting it is a perfect stopping place.

We left at around 8.30am in the pouring rain and took off to find another of our private roads. We began by driving the **N44** to **Vitry-le-François**, which is a dead-straight but busy highway. (Incidentally, at the right season of the year, all the farms along this route offer freshly picked asparagus – a tiny detour well worth making if you're on the way back).

The **N44** is not much fun to drive since outside Châlons-sur-Marne it is single carriageway and a favourite route for juggernauts. After about 16km it improves and becomes dual carriageway, though it is still very busy. Should you prefer a prettier drive, stay on this **N44** with

the juggernauts for company for 11km and then take the
D54 at the village of **Pogny**. This little road is on the right
a short way into Pogny. Once properly into the village you
must turn left again on to the **D2**. Watch out for the
signpost, as it is easy to go straight on by mistake. Once
on the **D2** you remain on it, passing pretty scenery and
spectacular silos. The French build their silos with a sort
of awesome grandeur. Some could pass for modern cathedrals. This road is quiet, a little twisty at the beginning,
but its virtue is that it bypasses Vitry-le-François.

If you find that the **N44** is not too busy and you are
making good progress, you can still cut out
Vitry-le-François by staying on the **N44** and turning right
(if going South) at the village of **Gravelines**, just 5km
from Vitry. Look out for the turning after dropping down
a long, steep hill. This little road, signposted to
Loisy-sur-Marne, takes you across to the **D2**.

Once in Loisy, look for the signpost on the left to
Maisons-en-Champagne. Keep your eyes peeled because
it is situated in a leafy hedge and easy to miss! This left
turn takes you on to the **D2**, where you turn left again
following the signposts to **Vitry**. Ahead is the **N4**, which
you cross straight over – the only tricky bit – and into the
scruffy little village of **Blacy**. The road then eventually
slides gently into the **D396** to **Brienne-le-Château** and on
to **Bar-sur-Aube**.

The **D396** is typically French, seemingly endless, often
treelined, straight as a yard of pumpwater and minus traffic, a ribbon of tarmac over the wide sweep of countryside.
We were much too early for lunch at the *Auberge de la
Plaine*, which sits in the middle of nowhere outside
Brienne-le-Château, but should you be looking for lunch
in this area (or indeed a bed) the *Plaine* is a decent,
straightforward little hotel, with no frills, extremely low
prices and good food.

At the *Angleterre* the night before Philip had been driving me mad channel-jumping with the TV but this irritating habit of his turned out to be fortuitous. In the middle
of his button-twiddling, we caught the tail-end of the
news. Here was the proud Minister of Transport, scissors
in hand, opening a new autoroute between Troyes and
Chaumont where it picks up with the Dijon/Beaune
motorway – what we think of as Our Autoroute, because

Brienne-
le-Château

we drove down it a couple of days after it opened some years ago. On our Michelin map for the area, this newly opened autoroute was sketched in, but no exits and entrances were marked. It lay about 12km below Bar-Sur-Aube, and if it were open, it would save us from taking the road through Colombey-les-Deux-Eglises and cut out the drive through Chaumont. Colombey, in spite of the de Gaulle connection (it was his home), is a boring little village, dominated by an over-the-top Cross of Lorraine erected to the General's memory.

'He might have been a tall man,' a friend of ours murmured on viewing this monolithic piece of stone looming over the landscape, 'but this is ridiculous!'

Chaumont

Though an awkward town to drive through, **Chaumont**, 27km down the road, is interesting to stop at since it has two awe-inspiring viaducts, which put the fear of God into Philip, who hates heights. But if we could pick up this brand new autoroute we could avoid both towns.

Bar-sur-Aube

As much as we like **Bar-sur-Aube**, a most pleasant little town where the river Aube rushes through and forms both a weir and a lake, it is a nuisance to get through – in spite of a one-way system. There was a time when we often stayed there, liking to walk by the river and enjoying the busy little high street. We also discovered a scruffy bar, misleadingly called *Le Royal*, full of equally scruffy but tranquil old gentlemen who go there to avoid the more modern bars, the pinball machines, the juke boxes and the leather-clad young. Not only can one find some peace and quiet in the *Royal*, one can also get a very good glass of champagne ridiculously cheaply. Just up the road was the *Hôtel Commerce*, an establishment where we stayed frequently, as Bar-Sur-Aube is just the right distance from Calais to catch an early afternoon boat home or to make a night stop coming from a morning boat. Fifteen years ago the *Commerce* was smart, with a good recommendation for food and a pleasant, busy restaurant. Alas, over the years the place went to pot and required a serious face-lift. The rooms became shabby, some rather beat-up, and therefore overpriced. The food had lost its lustre. A pity. We had liked to stay there as they had a lock-up courtyard but reluctantly decided enough was enough. Luckily for those who may have made the same decision, the charming old

building and rose-covered courtyard which housed the
Commerce has changed hands. The hotel is now called the
Relais des Gouverneurs and is run by Madame Guilleminot,
who has made considerable improvements. Under the new
management a double with shower costs around £24 a
night.

As we drove through Bar-sur-Aube it was still raining
in cords, as the French say, and just outside we took a
chance on finding the new autoroute by taking a D road –
the **D396** – which branches off to the right just south of
the town. The only clue that this might form a link was
that the road was signposted 'Dijon'. It rapidly became
clear that Something Was Up. Like the road. The last
time we had taken this route it had been a narrow little
lane, running through the up-and-down countryside. Now
it was a mass of gravel pits, piles of earth, machinery and
one-way sections, while a great many men worked frantically, laying new steaming tarmac, adding to the general
misty dampness of the morning. We agreed that this was
one of the few examples of road works where something
was actually happening. And, *voilà*, at the end of it all
there was a shiny new blue sign for the autoroute.

It was 10.15am, and the only snag with this brand new
entrance to the brand-new road was that it wasn't open.
Several cars and a couple of lorries were waiting at the
péage, but the ticket machines were not working and a line
of orange cones blocked the entrances towards both Paris
and Dijon. A police car, parked on the far side of the
cones, made sure no-one sneaked through.

I braved the pelting rain to ask the juggernaut driver at
the head of the queue if he knew what the problem was.
He was a stocky, friendly man with arms like hams and a
small brown nut of a face. He wore a funny German soldier's cap, no doubt picked up on his travels. He also had
a most extraordinary accent, which I had trouble deci-
phering. His vehicle number ended in 78 and, checking
this out later, I found out that he came from Les Landes,
near Bordeaux.

'Ah, madame,' he explained. 'They are late. The route
is intended to be open at 10 o'clock, but no-one has
arrived. It is necessary to wait for just a little while and
then we can all go.'

His smile said: Why didn't we have patience (not nor-

mally a French virtue), and all would be well. So we sat
and waited along with everyone else and, sure enough, at
about 10.30 a little yellow van came tearing along and out
leapt a young man – with the entry tickets. He and
another young man who had been pottering around the
booth began inserting the all-important tickets into the
distributor machine, the police drove off, the cones were
moved and we were nearly on our way – the third vehicle
to drive this new autoroute. But there was a hitch. The
distributor machine wasn't working properly and the man
from the yellow van handed us a ticket as we went by. I
was laughing and he laughed too.

'*Bonne route!*' he shouted after us. '*Soyez prudent*'. In
other words enjoy the drive and be careful.

This road, the **A5**, joins the **A31** and makes a huge loop
round **Dijon**, skirting places with thirsty-making names
like **Nuits-St-Georges**, before arriving at **Beaune** to pick
up the **A6**, which links with the **A7** and the **A8**. This is
the **Autoroute du Soleil** which eventually finishes up in
Italy. Not until Beaune is this autoroute particularly busy.
After that it can be a different story. Between Beaune and
Orange the road has to bear much of the traffic to Spain,
as well as that for the South of France. In high season it
can be a slow journey.

On our newly opened section of the **A5**, not surprisingly, we didn't see another car for the next 11km but the
rain was too heavy to go at any speed. And when we
passed the exit for Chaumont and began meeting heavy
lorries, driving became miserable. Though French autoroutes are magnificent, Philip has a theory that they hold
water more than British roads, with the result that passing
a huge, multi-wheeled lorry is like going through a particularly fierce and blinding bathroom shower. Even the
Mercedes' powerful windscreen wiper had to fight against
the volume of water. With Philip muttering that those
oversized lorries should be made to wear skirts, we battled
on, recalling our high hopes of what must be an experi-
mental section of autoroute between Nice and Cannes.
Here, on some kind of entirely different surface, the
lorries throw up barely any spray, even in a downpour.
Whatever it is, can we have it everywhere, please?

*

Into Wine Country

Nuits-St-Georges

Had it not been so early in the day, we might have given up, as the driving was so unpleasant. Indeed, it was tempting to do so, as this wine country has a good choice of stopping places. We are fond of an hotel just outside **Nuits-St-Georges** called *La Gentilhommière* in the valley of La Serrée. You come off the autoroute at the Nuits-St-Georges exit, drive through the little town for 1.5km on the Route Meuilley and there on the left is the hotel with its patterned tile roof and little Burgundian turrets. It is well off the road, down a rough drive that leads to the main building and a row of rooms converted from stables.

The main hotel is very smart, with an elegant restaurant – all beams, stone walls, pillars and a superb stone table centrepiece. It manages to be rustic yet upmarket and the large bar has a huge open fireplace. Converted from a 16th-century hunting lodge, the stable rooms are adequate though a little overpriced, since they are somewhat gloomy. The French can be awfully mean with electric light bulbs!

At the *Gentilhommière* the nicest bedrooms are within the hotel itself, but open the door of one of the ex-stables and you are in the country with a trout river running through the grounds and flocks of geese and goats roaming before your very eyes. It's all very bucolic, particularly in the morning when the guests are wakened by the alarming noise of geese squawking as breakfast is served to them. It sounds as if murder is being done. Murder most fowl, perhaps.

This is not a cheap hotel. Though the rooms are reason-ably priced, the restaurant is expensive. But it is ex-tremely good. The food borders on *nouvelle cuisine*, but without leaving one starving. As you might imagine, there is a fine wine list, though be prepared to be surprised at the prices. But it is such a charming room in which to dine – open fires, attentive service, and the look of an old castle. We recommend it.

If you can manage to reach Nuits-St-Georges around lunchtime, do stop. It is such a pretty town, and worth a look. In the very centre on a narrow street is the old town *beffroi* (belfrey), a charming, ivy-covered building. Right beside it is *Le Beffroi* café and I can't think of a nicer place to stop for a light lunch. It has outside tables sheltering under the walls of the belfry itself, and inside the café is really rather smart, done out in maroon stripes. Down one side are low seats set with tables for those who just want a drink and a sandwich, where they also serve a great *croque-monsieur* – a deep-fried sandwich of ham and cheese. When we visited *Le Beffroi*, we sat at the tables ranged along the other side, where, this time, I had a smashing ham omelette and Philip ordered *tripe à la mode de champagne* and ate every mouthful. It came with lots of fresh bread, a mountain of chips, mixed vegetables, half a bottle of rather special 1985 Nuits-St-George and mineral water – all for £17. A find.

But on our Autumn journey it was far too early to stop at *Le Beffroi*, and far too early even for lunch at our other favourite stopping-place, **Arc-sur-Tille**, a quiet little town minutes off the autoroute, where there is a particularly good roadside restaurant – *Le Poêlon*. It could not be more different from the *Gentilhommière*, set as it is in a large crumbling building on the main road. You enter from a side street. It's spacious, scruffy, and with the most wonderful seen-it-all, done-it-all oversized waitress who runs the place, ambling about on care-worn feet, with a permanent, patient smile on her face. The first time we stopped here, early at lunchtime, her fellow waiter had obviously been at the *vin blanc* since breakfast. The fellow's progress through the crowded restaurant, balancing a well-loaded tray, was pure suspense. Alas, several times he did not make it back to the bar, as the sounds of breaking glass testified. But no-one turned a hair. Locals, lorry-drivers, all of us just got on with a wonderful lunch under the benevolent eyes of the head waitress. There is no choice. We got what we were given. On our first visit it was a large plate of pâté with what I call a proper portion (lots!) of incredibly good baby pickled cucumbers, followed by a dish of rabbit served with rice and beans. This was followed by cheese – a great platter of it left for us to be as piggy as we liked, and then a dessert of ice cream or crème caramel. All excellent. The only thing that threw our slow-footed but sure waitress was our request for a bottle of wine. Must it be a bottle? she wanted to know. It

Arc-sur-Tille

all came in a bottle, she explained (presumably a very large one), but their method was to serve it in a carafe. So we settled for that, and though it was not a top-class burgundy it was very drinkable indeed. The whole meal set us back about £7 a head with coffee.

If such a basic atmosphere is not to your taste and you'd rather be given a choice of menu, there is another good, but classier, hotel restaurant in Arc-sur-Tille: *Les Marronniers d'Arc*. This is in the Route de Dijon, behind the *Poêle*. *Les Marronniers* has a charming garden where you can eat out in the summer, well-shaded, as you might guess, by *marronniers* – chestnut trees – and with some very unusual hand-made garden furniture, cast in heavy metal but looking like wood. All set out as it was, in front of the hotel, we realised why it is totally safe from the light-fingered. To move a piece would need a crane.

We very much liked this spacious, light hotel where the dining room is cool even on a hot day. The staff were young and shy, but willing. The speciality is fish, and the focal point of the room is a huge ornamental fish tank swimming with dinner – lobsters and crayfish. We left them to swim and both chose a plate of Mediterranean prawns with spicy rice. A bottle of excellent Aligoté was only just over £6. We followed all this with a sinful sweet – Phil had his usual chocolate mousse – and coffee. The *Marronniers* is not cheap – without a first course our bill was around £40, but I did indulge in a glass of champagne. You pay to some extent for surroundings, and here they are charming. Tables set wide apart, no irritating music, a nice gentle atmosphere in which to relax before hitting the road again. And luxury loos!

We have never managed to sleep at the *Marronniers*, but would have no hesitation doing so if the timing were right. It is extremely attractive, well-run and sparkling clean. Since the garden is geared to hold a great many people, there is a possibility that it might be busy, indeed noisy, on a warm summer night, but then one could join in the fun.

Arc-sur-Tille itself, incidentally, is a most pleasant little residential town with an air of prosperity about it. Should you need a meal and accommodation in this area of France, it makes more sense to stay here than to go on to the large town of Dijon unless, of course, you want to take

Dijon a look at this elegant old town. Dijon is easy to get lost in, is a long way off the autoroute and you can waste time if you are in a hurry – though it must be said that this town, made wealthy by wine and mustard, has a selection of grand hotels if you are looking for luxury. You can choose from *La Cloche* or the *Chapeau Rouge*, which has a star for food. Both are right in the town and both are first-class old French hotels.

Lunch Break

We continued on past both Arc-sur-Tille and Dijon as the rain continued to beat down. It was barely 12 o'clock, so we kept driving, stopping briefly at the *Aire Brognon*, where there is a good-sized Leclerc supermarket as well as a petrol station and restaurant. We wanted to buy a bottle of cassis for our favourite south of France drink, kir. Kir is made with a glass of good white wine with a slosh of cassis and it is a lovely sunshine drink. Kir Royale, made with champagne, is both nicer and more expensive. The *Aire Brognon* autoroute stop has a wonderful selection of cassis – an alcoholic blackcurrant juice which bears no relationship at all to Ribena. The cassis is made in Nuits-St-Georges and at 20% volume it has quite a kick. It is a sin to make a kir out of nasty cheap plonk in an attempt to hide the taste of the wine. The perfect kir is made with four-fifths of good Aligoté to one fifth of cassis, and, most important, is served well chilled. A Communard or a Cardinal is made by mixing the same proportions but using red burgundy.

Two bottles of cassis safe in the boot, we soldiered on. It was tiring, but Philip stuck it out until, at 1pm we came off the autoroute at **Mâcon Sud** and drove 2km along the

Crèches-sur-Saône
N6, stopping at the first village we came to. This was **Crèches-sur-Saône**, where we spotted an ordinary-looking brasserie right opposite a car park – conveniently placed for avoiding the rain.

We hadn't picked particularly well. A brasserie in France conjures up a picture of a large, cheerful warm room, with lots of people tucking into steak and chips. Brasseries should be busy and bustling (and we recom-

mend you to the *Brasserie de l'Est* opposite the Gare de
L'Est, should you ever be hungry in that area of Paris).
This one in Crèches-sur-Saône was not in the same class.
It was empty rather than bustling, and gloomy, with bare
wooden tables and chairs. About four other customers and
a rather timid elderly waitress were the only people present. We sat down and, since we were in the middle of
Beaujolais, ordered two glasses of wine – one white, one
red. I picked up my white and the smell hit me before I'd
even had a sip. The tolerant Philip, normally prepared to
give a glass of corked wine the benefit of the doubt,
agreed with me that it was definitely off and took the glass
back to the long bar. The barmaid was not best pleased
but she poured me a glass of red.

Unfortunately it is not true that you can't be served bad
wine – or indeed bad meals – in France. The very first
time that Philip and I drove south together we stopped in
Beaune for a quick snack lunch and ordered a small carafe
of the house plonk. I thought it was vile and refused to
touch it, but Philip who had got it into his head that we
were in Beaune and therefore it couldn't be *that* bad, continued to drink it. We stayed at the *Beau Rivage*, a
favourite hotel of mine on the west bank of the Rhône at
Condrieu that night. It has a star for food and is generally
rather special. Poor Philip was too ill to eat a mouthful. In
fact, he was quite poorly, poisoned, I am convinced, by
wine that wasn't Beaune at all but some chemical, nasty
Algerian red.

A decent restaurant will almost always have a decent
house wine, but some of the more snacky places do serve
rubbish, particularly when it comes served in one of those
ugly speckled pottery carafes that they make by the million at Vallauris, just up in the hills from Golfe-Juan down
in the South. When in doubt it is best to order a bottle.
Which, of course, is what we really should have done in
Crèches-sur-Saône. However, the place redeemed itself.
The menu was just under £5, for which we were given two
slices of mortadella with salad and a good pork chop with
creamed spinach and rice followed by *fromage blanc*.
Appearances aren't everything, though I must say that
Crèches-sur-Saône looked to be one of the less interesting
spots in Beaujolais. But perhaps this is an unfair judge-
ment, as still it poured dismally with rain.

The rain stopped us earlier that afternoon than we had intended. We wanted to get to Avignon, a town where we never get to stay the night, but it was just too far with the weather conditions being so poor. We had been given a taste for exploring Avignon on a journey back in the September of 1990. We had spent the night in the Camargue and moved on to Arles – Van Gogh country. From there we drove along the quiet west bank of the Rhone (**D15, D2**). It was an interesting, though far from beautiful route, that passed wide stretches of river, scrubby countryside, vineyards and orchards interspersed with heavy industry and vast power stations. It is only worth driving if you are bored with the autoroute and wanting to avoid the heavy traffic on the **N7**. The road led into **Villeneuve-les-Avignon**, which sits on the Rhône on the opposite bank to Avignon itself.

'It'll be a horrid little new town, I expect,' I warned as we neared. But not a bit of it. Although called Villeneuve – New Town – it looks as if it has been there since time began, and is guarded by the ancient Fort St André, which looms over the town and looks out over the Rhône.

'It must have been new once,' pointed out Philip.

But a long, long time ago. Villeneuve-les-Avignon is ancient, spectacular and charming, and we were dipped in luck in that we arrived on a bright Saturday morning when the town market was in progress on a large expanse of land right under the castle walls.

There are markets and markets. I love our little Grasse market, situated by a fountain surrounded by flower-sellers. The big covered market in Cannes, open every morning, is another joy. The Saturday market in Dieppe has a lot going for it, with the country-folk arriving from their Normandy farms to sell their butters and cheeses, all in hand-carved chunks. All French markets are pleasing, but never have I seen one to match the market at Villeneuve-les-Avignon. For a start, it is enormous. It takes a good hour to wander its length if the merchandise is to be given the attention it deserves. There are old clothes and new clothes at the far end, and a sprinkling of arts and crafts stalls, but this market is basically into the serious business of eating. The fruit and the vegetables, wonderful fresh breads of all kinds and local olive oils and herbs, are sold from wooden stalls. Each of the stalls is a

cornucopia of riches of the South: glistening black figs, fat
sweet-scented melons, fuzzy peaches, lush bunches of
black and green grapes all piled in careless, inviting profusion. And the vegetables! Perfect little carrots and auber-
gines, green beans, leeks, swollen golden onions and beer-
bellied cauliflowers against the bright and beefy tomatoes
of Provence. But nothing allowed to get so big that the
flavours are lost. Some stalls sell great jars of honey-
coloured or greeny olive oil, cheek by jowl with all kinds
of pickled olives and onions, dried fruits (the dried
apricots are irresistible) and God knows what else, side by
side with the crusty bread, teased into all kinds of shapes
and baked with different types of flour. A market bounti-
ful beyond measure.

Meat, fish, *charcuterie*, cheeses and *pâtisserie* were set up
on magnificent trailers which opened up into full-sized
shops. These trailers are commonplace in France. We
once had such a vehicle in our local Grasse market, a small
and elderly one, owned by an apple-cheeked lady who sold
cheeses, butter and the odd bits of grocery. Alas, her
husband became ill and she now cares for him instead of a
cheese-loving public. In Villeneuve-les-Avignon there
were dozens of these mobile stores, each one grander than
the last. The place was maddening in that I wanted to buy
everything I saw, but we still had two days on the road.
The one thing I did need and which would have kept –
wine vinegar – did not appear to be on sale. Perhaps the
Côte du Rhône wines are too good for making vinegar.

We had promised ourselves we would return to
Avignon to see if old Avignon was as charming as the
new. But with the rain beating down this was not the
time. I have a tried and tested theory that the weather
changes at Lyon, but on this occasion it was not working.
Nine times out of 10 the theory holds. If it's pelting and
chilly in Beaujolais, once we have driven through Lyon,
more often than not the sun is shining on the soft green
hills of the Côte du Rhône and glittering on the broad
sweep of the river. One March I left Villefranche, just
north of Lyon, in a blizzard and found the sun shining in
Vienne, just south. And the same can apply coming
North. Bad weather along the Rhône valley will brighten
in Beaujolais. But not this time. So we settled for staying
at **Montélimar**, a Provence town famous for its nougat.

Imperial Refuge

I had stayed in **Montélimar** once before in the days BP (before Philip) when I used to drive myself South alone. I had been coming back in July 1980, had left it too late before stopping and was trying to find an hotel with a vacancy in the beautiful Drôme countryside. But there was no room at any inn.

In those days, when in the car alone, I would feel a kind of mild panic when there was no accommodation to be found, and I knew that the best bet was to head for the nearest large town. Somewhere there must be a bed for rent in a big town. And the nearest was Montélimar.

I found refuge at the *Relais de l'Empereur* – not the cheapest spot, but one where there was at least a vacancy. I was so tired that I remember little about my room, but I do remember that everyone was truly kind. As a woman on my own I was given the best seat in the restaurant – where I could see everyone and they could see me (in Britain and the USA a woman alone is tucked out of sight behind a pillar). The food was *nouvelle cuisine* at a time when *nouvelle cuisine* really was new. I am not truly a devotee of this kind of cooking and not sorry to see it losing favour. As our friend Vivienne Glenavy says, one doesn't know whether to eat it or photograph it, but on this occasion any food was welcome.

That overnight stay had left me with warm feelings about the *Relais de l'Empereur*, and we decided to go back, particularly when we realised that the hotel was a 'Best Western'. The Best Western hotels where we have stayed generally have a faded charm and seem to be run by pleasant people. I had always been puzzled at their individuality – one has nothing in common with another – until Bini Tuxen, a German friend in the hotel business, explained that Best Western, like the *Relais de Silence* group, are not truly a chain. They are a group of independent hotels who have joined together to share a central booking agency and promotional costs. This is obviously a good idea for the hotelier, but from the customer's point of view one cannot be entirely sure of the amenities that are on offer. They can vary considerably. But Best Western hotels are neither plastic nor predictable, which gives them a certain appeal just as, in our experience, the *Relais de Silence* hotels are tranquil places to stay.

As we came off the autoroute at Montélimar Nord my vague memories of the town were of a long, straight street selling little else but nougat.

'Nice hotel, boring town,' I told Philip, who by this time didn't care too much where we went, as long as we stopped driving. I was to be proved wrong again.

The *Relais de l'Empereur*, a large, imposing, white building, was where I had left it – on the Place Marx Dormoy. The entrance is at the side, where there is a garden and a large area for parking. If you are a light sleeper it is best to ask for a room on this quiet side, as the ring road around Montélimar runs along the other side.

Our first impressions were good. An attractive woman popped out of the hotel door as soon as our car stopped, ready to greet us. She was rapidly followed by another woman, who took the baggage, led us to our room and turned down the beds. The large lobby, the white marble staircase and the corridor to our room were full of Napoleonic memorabilia, busts, paintings, tapestries and a lot of laurel wreaths with an 'N' in the middle. Had you wondercd even for a moment which *Empereur* the hotel was named after, one second inside its doors revealed all.

Our bedroom was large. It also had a small sitting room with a television behind draped curtains and an ancient, noisy but efficient bathroom. Alas, the bed hangings were faded, the curtains off their hooks and the expensive wallpaper had seen better days. The beds were comfortable. We felt, though, that it was a little overpriced at £58.

The town turned out to be a pleasant surprise when we went for our *petite promenade* before dinner. Just across from the hotel was the entrance into the old town – a long, part-pedestrian street of very good shops. The burghers of Montélimar have been clever. They have encased their old town safely within the ring road, so that it is barely spoilt by the thundering traffic of the N7. The Rhône runs right through the centre of the town, flanked by stone walls, and there is an air of prosperity about the place. Can it come from selling the ubiquitous nougat? Every other shop displays the stuff and the town smells, not unpleasantly, of it. Naturally, we bought some – at nearly £2 for a small slab. Maybe that *is* where the prosperity comes from.

We had our before-dinner baths, trying to control the bath plug, which made the most extraordinary noise and sounded like a demented machine gun as the water ran away. And then we went down to the bar for a drink.

Henri, a cheerful, balding fellow who had obviously been with the hotel man and boy, served us before leaving us to the mercies of his assistant, a large, dark, lowering man who seemed to be adding up figures. His forehead was almost impossibly low. We attempted the odd friendly remark and got not so much as a grunt in return. Determined to beat my way through this wall of indifference, since we were the only customers, I smiled. He stared stonily back. To break the icy silence, Philip set about translating a wooden wall plaque containing the sort of words of wisdom that amuse the French hugely. This one told us that men were like melons – the riper they were, the better they were.

'Très sage,' I said chattily – if not very accurately – to the barman, who merely acted as if I wasn't there.

He did smile in the end. That was when we got up to go: tipping time. Too late! Too late! And we were amused when we found an even larger, even grumpier wine waiter in the restaurant. They had to be brothers.

But the head waiter made up for both of them. Monsieur Marc was eager to please. He, too, had lost his hair in the service of the hotel. He had joined in 1954, back in the days of the *Empereur*'s glory. Monsieur Marc had a soft spot for the British. He explained how he had been just 16 when the war began and how he had drifted around Europe with the British and American forces. He kept telling us that it was in these years that he had perfected his English. Since he always used the royal 'we' when talking about himself, this made the drift of his conversation difficult to follow.

'There where you are sitting,' he said, pointing a dramatic finger, 'was where we myself always served Sir Anthony Eden. A great gentleman. And at that table before you, we myself served Richard Burton and Mrs Burton, and,' he added triumphantly, 'Elizabeth Taylor.' Questioning revealed that, yes, it was all three of them at once.

It seemed that the owner of the hotel had worked for many years in Claridges, and because of the connections he had made there, Winston Churchill had been a regular at the *Empereur*. Presidents of France had passed through the portals. Looking at the large vase of dead gladioli on the centre serving table, I reflected that things weren't what they used to be – though probably the prices were similar. Three lamb chops for £14 seemed a little steep. Whereas on the previous night we would not have complained if they had charged more, we could not truthfully say the same for the *Empereur*. And yet on paper both hotels had the same qualifications. It just goes to show something or other. Probably that it's a long time since a Michelin inspector visited the *Relais de l'Empereur*. But if you like faded glory and memories of times past, the overall atmosphere of *L'Empereur* is sympathetic.

Home Run

The following morning the sun shone. We were at Les Eygages well in time for lunch with our neighbours. That last stretch of motorway over the mountains is always a joy. In the late Autumn, on a good day, there is a clarity to the air which makes every last lump, hump and bump along the mountain ridges stand out in sharp relief. The colours are deepened. The grey rock of Mount Ste Victoire, Cézanne's favourite subject, snatches white from great fluffs of cloud. The mountains of Roquebrun are truly chocolate brown, the last of the vines on the hillsides a wonderful gold or glowing russet. The sky itself is as innocently blue as an infant's eyes. With most of the visitors gone and the locals having time to chat, it is a perfect time to explore.

Our stay lasted a little under a week. We arrived to find that Les Eygages had two new babies. Our neighbour opposite, Monique, had produced a girl, Marie, just four weeks previously. We had seen Monique last in September, looking bonny but enormous with just a week or so to go; a dark, smiling mother-earth-in-waiting. Now she was slender as a wand and looking wonderfully *chic*.

Her husband, Michel, who sells paper for a living and is a truly happy man, always smiling and singing, was bursting with pride. Marie was a veritable princess, he informed us. The beautiful blonde Olga, who lives behind us and up the hill with her suave husband, Jean-Pierre, was still in hospital with her two-day-old son, Dimitri. She came home the day we left and alas, we never got to see the baby at that time.

'*Faites attention!*' said Jean, as he imparted the news of this rash of births. 'Les Eygages has a microbe!'

'In my case it wouldn't be a microbe but a miracle,' I told him.

'Non! Non! Non!' he said, gallantly French as ever.

Magagnosc

Our English neighbours, Dick and Kath, having given us lunch when we arrived, gave us lunch when we left the following Saturday at midday at our favourite simple little restaurant, the *Petite Auberge* at **Magagnosc**, on the route to Grasse. Though it is an inexpensive restaurant, serving good honest food, they have a trout tank on their terrace, and they offer *truite au bleu* on the menu.

Now the only way, alas, to enjoy the perfect *truite au bleu* is for the unfortunate fish to be dropped, alive, into boiling water. It curls up – as well it might – and cooks instantly. I am not proud of it, but I love *truite au bleu*, presented with just some melted butter and boiled potatoes. It is undoubtedly one of the world's great dishes, but Philip says I am cruel to order it, and he's probably right.

The Return Journey

Comfortably full of trout and apricot tart, we set off around 1.30pm. We planned to take the same route, but of course, having left at a different time, we would find ourselves brand new stopping places. Philip's plan was to drive 200 miles on the Saturday afternoon, 400 miles on the Sunday, since there would be hardly any heavy traffic, and 200 more miles to finish the journey on Monday morning before catching the boat. Four hundred miles may sound a lot of driving for sensible drivers in one day, but the autoroutes out of season are quiet and it is perfectly possible. Actually, if conditions were good, we told ourselves, it would be a nice, leisurely journey.

But unwittingly we had broken one of our own rules – never to drive in France on the last (or first) weekend of a month.

We hadn't considered it a problem because, somehow, the first weekend in November didn't seem like a time when a lot of tourists would be about. But neither had we taken into account *Toussaint* (All Saints), one of the many French national holidays, which had taken place on the Thursday.

By the Sunday of *Toussaint* there was a lot of traffic on the road. Mostly Parisian cars, belting like lunatics back North along with a great many Belgians, who can be equally lunatic. There were also a lot of German and Dutch cars pulling caravans back home for the winter, so the road was busy. We lost most of the Germans at Vienne, just before Lyon, where they nip off to the East, and the remainder vanished on the autoroute to Geneva at Mâcon. The Parisians hogged the road until Beaune and the Belgians and the Dutch were always with us.

Where to stay the night? A bank holiday weekend could pose an accommodation problem. There are all sorts of places you can dart off to in Provence if you start driving in the early afternoon. The area is full of possibilities. During our previous trip in September we had decided to take a look at the mouth of the Rhône at **Port-Saint-Louis**, on the other side of Marseilles which is, I suppose, technically the Languedoc. It was a glorious late summer evening with the sun low in the sky making great shadows on the mountains. We took the autoroute past Aix-en-Provence and came off at Salon-de-Provence and set off in the direction of Arles before turning on to the **N113** towards St-Martin-de-Crau.

It is curious countryside in this part of Provence; near enough to being bleak, dramatic if you happen to be the sort of person who gets great joy from a view of the Battersea Power Station. There is a lot of inland water which, unless the sun is shining brilliantly, only manages to look surly. Huge chemical works dominate the wide skyline and there are monotonous areas of the kind of grim wasteland that the French call *terrain vague*. It is interesting in an off-beat kind of way, but it wasn't what we had imagined. It took a lot of map-reading to get on to the road to Port-Saint-Louis and I was wondering if it was worth it. The scenery was mostly depressing, looking more like some unloved spot in middle America than Provence. Eventually we saw Port-Saint-Louis in the distance – grey and blocklike. Though we may well have done the town a serious injustice we made a snap decision that this was not for us and instantly swerved to the right on to a much narrower, equally straight road.

'We'll go to the Camargue and see the white horses instead,' I said.

These instant decisions don't allow much time for map-reading. I was desperately trying to sort out exactly where we were (which was on the **D35**) when Phil said, 'We're coming to some place called Bac.'

'Can't find it on the map,' I muttered frantically.

It was rather shaming to find that, in all the years I have gone through France, this was the first time I had ever come across the word *Bac* – which simply means ferry. Shortly afterwards the road ran out and we found ourselves with nowhere else to go except on to a waiting boat. The ferry man, who must have seen us coming from miles back in this featureless landscape, had waited and was impatiently beckoning us aboard. Once we were in place and had paid our tiny toll we chugged over a narrow part of the Rhône and were deposited in a small town called **Salin de Giraud**. Here things instantly improved.

Lucky Diversion

We were in the Camargue and driving up the **D36** in the direction of Arles, leaving the sea behind us. The Camargue is something of an acquired taste: board-flat, water everywhere, hedges of sugar cane, fields of rice and of solid black bulls drifting in herds making strong shapes against the endless sky. There's hardly any habitation. The wind whistles and crackles in the sugar cane and turns a field of long grass into a sea of waves. The winds pervade the place most of the time and after a while it becomes easy to understand why its constant, unfocused wail drove Van Gogh to cut off his ear. But there's beauty here and a fascination that's impossible to deny. In high summer the prevailing colour is gold. Gold from the sunflowers, the ripening crops and the sun. Even the sky can look like molten gold. But the fabled white horses and the flamingoes are shy and not keen to show themselves for the tourist. If you wish to see the wildlife, it really is necessary to go on horseback and, whatever you do, don't forget the mosquito repellant. Camargue mosquitos could double for vampires. They can draw your blood even through a sweater.

Le Sambuc

We decided to head for the *Longo Maï* hotel in the village of **Le Sambuc**, 13km from the ferry. There wasn't another car on the narrow, dead-straight road which ran through vast rice estates and it took no time at all. Which was as well, since the journey from leaving the autoroute and getting to the *Bac* was one neither of us would care to drive again.

Le Sambuc looks like a refugee from the Wild West and we instantly warmed to it. The village has a wide main street with just one row of small buildings on either side. It is dusty, with an air of impermanence, as if the wind might one day blow it into the Etang du Berre – the Camargue's whopping great lake. The hotel, a long, low, cream-painted building with seven white horses tethered outside under shade, sits on the edge of the village. The buildings are surrounded by a wattle fence. At the side of the hotel is a small bullring where, we were told, 'fun' bullfights were held. Fights where no one, certainly not the bull, got hurt.

It seemed the horses must be left loose a lot of the time. We picked our way through evidence of their presence and received a warm welcome from Monsieur Raynaud, the owner of the hotel. Tall and willowy, in tight jeans and a floppy shirt, he had the long black hair, beaky face and deep-set black eyes of a gypsy. He could have been from one of the tribes who visit Stes-Maries-de-la-Mer in the Camargue for their festival every May. We persuaded ourselves that maybe he was, but he turned out to be a Parisian!

He showed us a room off an open terrace in a separate brick building at the side of the main hotel. It was small

but adequate with a nice little bathroom and cost about
£35. We noted that they had been thoughtful enough to
leave a can of mosquito repellant, even though the windows and doors were swathed in heavy mosquito netting.
Croaking for a drink, we dropped our luggage and went to
sit in the garden that surrounded the hotel.

We had just been served our beers and I was gratefully
swallowing mine when Phil said quietly, 'Don't jump.
There's a horse about to put its head on your shoulder.'

At that moment a heavy nose landed near my ear and
snuffled about a bit. Turning somewhat cautiously, I
found myself gazing into the long-lashed brown eyes of a
heavily pregnant white mare. She snorted, turned away
and continued to mooch round the garden, delicately
picking up fallen fruits.

We loved the hotel. Madame Raynaud is an animal
lover and she has 25 cats and one dog, who is there under
the cats' sufferance and spoilt rotten by the humans. The
walls were covered with surreal paintings of white horses
and unicorns, fairy princesses with yards of golden hair
and flaming red Camargue sunsets. They were not exactly
to our taste, but beautifully executed and romantic in the
extreme. The painter was our gypsy-looking host.

The Raynauds' son was there on holiday from London
and served our supper of a sturdy Provençal beef stew. He
sat down and chatted to us about his life in London.
Amazingly, he was the head waiter at *Mustard's*, a restaurant in Smithfield, not two miles from where we live.

Favourite Places

It would have been fun to have gone back to the *Longo
Maï* for a second reasonably priced stay but we decided it
would be a better spot to visit when coming from the
North, where it is simple to take the direct route from
Arles. So if we weren't going to the Camargue this time,
where were we going?

In the end we continued on the autoroute, coming off
at **Loriol**, in the Drôme, where I had spotted a little clus-
ter of small towns, all of which supported a decent hotel.

Working on the theory that at least one of them might
have room, we decided to stop in that area – which
pleased me, as the Drôme is almost my favourite part of
France.

In fact, I love the Drôme so much that I am forever
muttering that one day we should make a point of actually
living there for a while. The Côte d'Azur is wonderful,
glamorous, beautiful, irresistible, with everything possible
to offer, but somehow it is not *real* France.

The Drôme is quite as beautiful as the South of France
but in a less splashy way. It is much quieter and more
peaceful; there's not a lot going on. Philip points out,
quite rightly, that we might well be bored to death there.
But never by the views. The Drôme has vast fields of
sunflowers – or *tournesols* (turn to the sun), as the French
call them – marshalled in extravagant yellow rows, reflect-
ing and staring into the sunlight. The mountain sides are
smothered with lavender in every imaginable shade – from
deep, deep purple to pale lilac. Here are the orchards of
France, fruit trees bowed down by cherries, plums,
peaches and apricots, and, of course, always the vines. I
know no more wonderful sight than the vineyards of
Gigondas at evening time, when the sun catches and turns
the big round stones in which the vines are planted into
oversized, glittering jewels. These stones hold the warmth
of the day, ripening the grapes even in the cool of the
night, and producing the deepest red, heady wine with a
good night's sleep in every bottle. Behind the flat plains
where the vines and the orchards grow is the spectacular
backdrop of the Alps, looking near enough to toddle to in
the clear air. And this Autumn, the mountains were
already snow-capped – which we decided must be good for
skiers, since the previous winter France had had hardly
any snow at all.

Mirmande   The village of **Mirmande**, where we headed first, is just
6km off the autoroute. Leave the autoroute at Loriol and
take the **N7** South, being careful to look for the sign for
Mirmande (3km) on the left (**D204**). Three long kilometres, Philip noted. At first the road is flat and in the
distance, perched and tumbling on a lonely peak, is a
small, ancient village. Then the road begins to climb and
it becomes obvious that Mirmande is higher than you
think. We were heading for a hotel called *La Capitelle*,

59

which turned out to be a 17th-century, beautifully mellow stone building, set high on the 5th-century ramparts and staring out across a view of meadows, mountains and orchards.

We parked in the village car park and walked up the hill to the hotel. At the side of the small entrance hallway beyond a wide arch was a big, comfortably furnished, low-ceilinged sitting room with squashy sofas and with a log fire burning in an oversized fireplace. A man at a small desk in the corner of the room rose to greet us. And yes, they had a room.

What a room it was. Spacious, extremely well-furnished with antique pieces, and a view across plain, hills and mountains, the like of which is hard to find. More practically, there was a modern bathroom and separate lavatory. The price was just over £50 a night. It was aptly a *Relais de Silence*, for Mirmande is one of the most tranquil villages imaginable, without being moribund, as some French hill villages can be.

We went for our usual *petite promenade*. To explore Mirmande it helps if you are wearing flat, preferably rubber-soled shoes and if you haven't spent a week making a pig of yourself on French food. By the time we had clambered to the top of the village over a variety of surfaces – cobbles, rough stones, pebbles and the occasional concreted slope where the road was in danger of collapsing, I was so breathless I couldn't speak. But the view! Below, to the West, the Rhône wound through the countryside below the Ardèche Mountains. To the South was a panorama of pines and the mountains of Marsanne, and to the West the Vivarais Mountains. The village itself is all alleys – *ruelles*, as the French call these narrow streets. Alleys and arches and amazing ancient stone houses, beautifully restored – though some, temptingly, still need attention, causing Philip to ask the question that is unfailingly aired when he finds somewhere he particularly likes: 'I wonder if we could afford a little place here?'

Yet only 30 odd years ago, in the 1960s, the village of Mirmande was a total ruin. From being an important centre in the 17th century with a peaceful and prosperous community of artisans and, later, a silk centre, it was in total decline. The coming of artificial fabrics had put the community out of business and the people left the village to find work in the valleys. Those who stayed found life hard, and early in the century, in order to lessen their taxes, began taking layers of tiles from their roofs. Whereas Britain had a window tax in the 18th century, the French suffered a roof tax. Even now in the South people are judged for wealth on how many layers of the curved, terracotta tiles of Provence make up their roofs. One layer equals a sniff from the neighbours. Three or four snugly fitting one into the other smell of money. (Les Eygages has three!)

Mirmande was restored by the arrival of the painter, André Lhote. He stumbled across the sleeping village, fell in love with its tranquillity and created an Academy of Painting there. He bought and restored the building that is now *La Capitelle*, and his students snapped up the other ruins, paying a price determined by how many tiles were left on the roofs. They paid so little for the houses that when the Second World War disturbed the peace of Europe the school of painting closed and the students just left. They shut the great wooden doors, walked out and never came back. The village returned to crumbling sleep until the 1960s, when it was discovered again by townsfolk looking for second homes somewhere quiet and beautiful. The houses have been restored by Parisians, manufacturers from Lyon, and maybe even rich nougat makers from nearby Montélimar. It is a village of *residences secondaires* and therefore busy only in the summer months and at weekends. There is a resident potter, an elegant dress shop, and honestly not a lot else except a few cafés. We were very taken by the *Margot* – a perfect French café, not too scruffy not too smart. The posters on the wall were originals from the 1920s, the atmosphere relaxed, with the locals drinking *pastis* served by an agreeable young barman. Philip, after his half-litre of good blonde beer, announced that he could spend a lot of time sitting there and we wished we had had time to try their *cuisine à l'ancienne*.

We could not fault *La Capitelle*. Our evening meal was first class in a restaurant that was busy and yet managed to remain peaceful. The menus were by no means overpriced. More importantly, the food was excellent. It is a most agreeable hotel in a charming spot. The bill, with drinks before dinner and breakfast served in our room, was £100. One nice little touch – with our breakfast we were served half a locally grown kiwi fruit, set in an egg-cup! We give the *Capitelle* full marks, and next time we might even stay two nights.

After our kiwi-fruit breakfast we were on our way on a bright and sunny morning by 8.30am. Getting back onto the autoroute was quick and easy, but we found the traffic was still surprisingly heavy for November. We stopped to buy wine in a village in the Côte Chalonnais and, our purchase made, it was nearing one o'clock and we were hungry.

Chagny

It seemed sensible to stop at **Chagny**, just a kilometre or two up the road. Chagny is a pleasant Burgundy town and, once again, we had arrived on market day. The narrow main street of the town was blocked by stalls – in fact, it seemed as if the most of the town had been turned into a market for the day. Most of the stalls were already packed up, others still putting their wares into small vans, and the town dust-carts hovered waiting to clear up the market debris.

We set off to look for lunch, but the question was – how much lunch? Philip is still waiting to try his first three-star Michelin meal, and Chagny has one of the 16 three-star restaurants in France. Called the *Lameloise*, it sits, white-painted and grand, on the Place d'Armes facing down the main street. Should we or shouldn't we? But somehow a really splendid meal at lunchtime when travelling only serves to dampen the appetite for the evening meal. It is in the evening, after a bath and the *petite promenade*, when the luxury and relaxation of a meal is more valued. We decided against the *Lameloise* and instead took our custom to its humbler neighbour, the *Café Bourguignon*, just across the road. There, steak and chips and omelettes were on offer.

Should you ever be in Chagny and fancying an omelette, let us recommend you to the *Café Bourguignon*. There once was a time when one always got a wonderful omelette in France. That time is, sad to say, no more. That very week in a café in Cannes we had toyed with what could only be described as beaten-up fried egg.

'Maybe they tell the chef when the customer is British, and the chef thinks fried egg is what the British want,' Philip suggested gloomily as he pushed away his plate.

One fares better in the country. Dick and Kath were once served a poem of a 14-inch omelette in a tiny café in the village of Billy in the Loire, produced by a rather cross woman who was waiting to shut up shop and muttering imprecations as she thrust it before them. Her irritation had not affected the perfection of her skill with the omelette pan. At the *Café Bourguignon* our omelettes were golden brown on the outside, melting yellow inside and full of lovely ham. (If you like them wet and dribbly, as we do, you ask for them to be made *baveux*). These golden delights cost no more than a couple of beers. We were glad that we had decided the *Lameloise* could wait and wondered if, since a three-star establishment was only paces away, Monsieur Alain, proprietor of the *Bourguignon*, felt he had to try harder.

As simple as Monsieur Alain's establishment was, the idea is not as idiotic as it sounds. In France good restaurants are inclined to spawn, one around the other. An example is the little town of Talloires, on Lac Annecy, where there are nine recommended hotels and restaurants – one, *Auberge du Père Bise*, with two stars. Or an even better example: Mougins, on our own doorstep in the South, where a small hilltop village supports a three-star restaurant, the *Moulin des Mougins*, and two one-stars, as well as a gourmet's delight of other well-run, excellent establishments.

We were heading for a one-star ourselves that night. We had remembered a little hotel, the *Cheval Blanc* in Champagne at a village called **Sept-Saulx**, where we had tried to get in before and never been lucky. We thought we might try again. We took the brand new autoroute for a little longer on the way back, but avoided going the full distance into Troyes. The road from Troyes to Chaumont, the **N19**, is to be avoided at all costs. Though it is straight, with occasional patches of dual carriageway, it is also bogged down with vast lorries and heavy traffic, including farm equipment. It looks so good on the map – straight as a die across the plains – but every time we are lulled into travelling on it, there are regrets and grumbles all the way. Instead we came off the autoroute at the exit for **Vendeuvre-s-Barse**, taking the **D443** to **Brienne-le-Château**. Again we were a little too early for another favourite stopping place at **Bar-sur-Seine** – just

Bar-sur-
Seine

63

Bar-sur-Seine
10km to the South of this exit of the autoroute. It is worth the small detour to visit this sleepy, over-sized village on the river. For one thing it is peaceful. It sinks into slumber at around 9pm with barely a car to be heard. In the Place de la République there is a small, pleasant hotel called the *Hôtel du Commerce*, which is highly recommended if funds are running short. They always seem to give us room No. 1. This has a double bed, a single bed and a separate room with another single bed, plus a cot for the baby we don't have. With it comes a large, echoing separate loo, as well as a shower and washbasin with a long window that looks out over the main square. The curtains barely meet to hide one's modesty.

As the room only costs us around £18 for the night we have never bothered to say that we do not need all that accommodation. But this is another little French wrinkle to watch for. Hoteliers always, quite sensibly, unload their most expensive room first. If you find yourself being offered the family room and there are only two of you, or the best room in the house, ask firmly for something smaller and cheaper.

The *Hôtel du Commerce*, run by Madame Puissant and her chef husband, is amazing value. They have a good £5 menu, though we went for the £9, which gave Philip *escargots* and a plate of excellent duck. I chose a salad of gizzards and then pike, followed, of course, by the plateau of cheese and then dessert – chocolate mousse and strawberries. We did not stint ourselves on the wine and our bill, after a breakfast of still warm bread and very good coffee, was £55 for the night. Though the rooms are basic in the extreme, there is a small, pleasant bar off the lobby and, out of season, the large restaurant usually has a big log fire burning in the open grate. It's very country and comfortable and rather better decorated than most inexpensive French restaurants. We never mind the bedroom being basic; you can soon shut your eyes on it till morning. But it is pleasing to eat in more salubrious surroundings.

The *Commerce* was not for us that night. We had made up our minds to get back to Champagne and one star. The weather deserted us as soon as we reached the **N44** between Châlons-sur-Marne and Reims. While we were looking for the **D37** for **Sept-Saulx** (we found it on the right and very clearly marked, almost impossible to miss) the sky became very ominous indeed. Above our head was a thick black raincloud, and to the left, where the sun was going down over the vast flat bread basket that is Champagne, the horizon was red-streaked, dominated by a gigantic blood-red sun that appeared to have a paler red deep frill around its circumference. It hung so low in the angry sky that it looked about to fall. It was the strangest sunset either of us has ever seen. We have both witnessed the weird 'green flash' in the Caribbean when the sun goes down, but this was even more awe-inspiring – indeed, a little frightening. The effect of all that blood spattered in the sky was strange and alien, as if something momentous was about to happen.

Sept-Saulx   But all that occurred was more rain and fortunately the *Cheval Blanc* had a room for us. Again at much the same price we had been paying during the entire trip – around £50 for the night. It was an extremely pleasant room: large, immaculate, with twin beds. Beyond was a sitting room with television and mini bar, and beyond again, a large bathroom. The furnishings were a touch regal – lots of plum velvet – and our windows looked out to a large garden with both a stream and a river running through it. Well worth the price, though almost wasted for a one night stay.

The village of Sept-Saulx, apart from the *Cheval Blanc*, hasn't much to offer. It is a boring little spot and would not be a good place to be stuck for any length of time. But it was dark when we arrived, gone six, and we didn't particularly want to go anywhere. We smartened up and went down to dinner at the restaurant, which is across the road from the hotel. Fortunately the rain had stopped. Perhaps when it is raining they provide an umbrella.

The restaurant was very smart: *très distingué*, very well run, but it would have been perfectly at home in Paris, London or New York. It didn't seem to have a lot to do with a small Champagne village. Or that would have been the case except for the majority of the diners. There was a great band of men eating – probably around 30 of them – some of them dressed in ancient anoraks, shooting socks, boots, old flannel or cord trousers. Others were immaculate in Scottish tweed shooting jackets, smartly polished walking shoes and Argyle shooting socks, mixed in with those who wore a rag-bag of ancient but warm clothing. They were a curious lot and looked decidedly out of place in among the fine linen and crystal.

They were also making a lot of noise and we, along with the few other English and American guests, were placed outside the large restaurant in a smaller area, where it was quieter. There we enjoyed a pleasant but, I thought, unremarkable meal. If I had had to choose between the *Cheval Blanc* and the *Capitelle* and pronounce who deserved the star, the *Capitelle* would have been the runaway winner.

We also had to admit that it would have been a very airy, almost empty restaurant without the 30 men.

'They are, of course, a shooting party?' I said to the waiter. He raised his eyes to the ceiling.

'But yes,' he said. 'They were here at eight for the breakfast, now they have returned from the fields, taken an aperitif and now they dine.'

One of the better dressed men, whom we reckoned was picking up what must have been an astronomic bill, finally made a speech and they all went home, trooping through the restaurant in their boots. The waiters followed them, staggering under the weight of trays and trays of empty glasses. It was something, we decided, that would not have happened in Britain. Anyone wealthy enough to run a shoot that size would have taken his guests home to dine. But surely not the beaters as well? France, perhaps, is more democratic than we are.

It was not the first time that we have encountered curious groups in Champagne. We came across another at the

Ambonnay

village of **Ambonnay**, which is set on the other side of the autoroute. Ambonnay is a much pleasanter village than Sept-Saulx. It is well cared for – almost pretty by Champagne standards, where the villages are inclined to be a bit utilitarian. In Ambonnay every other house seems to produce its own champagne in honey-coloured brick establishments. It has one small hotel, the *Auberge St Vincent*, run by an energetic, friendly young couple who speak enough English to sort out anyone with no French. The uncompromising-looking hotel is fun because it is also the meeting place for the village. Therefore there is always a lot going on.

We had gone down to dinner in the big, old-fashioned

restaurant one night to find that one half of it had been screened off. We saw why when suddenly a group of about 50 ancient men and women marched in. I say 'marched' advisedly. The men, most of whom were well over 70, if not notching 80, wore chestfuls of medals and a collection of strange, military-style caps and berets. Many of them were Americans wearing old-fashioned violently checked jackets. It became apparent that these were men who had fought in Champagne in the last war. The Frenchmen were all 'ancient combatants', and were hosting a reunion dinner for their allies of so long ago. And with both Americans and Frenchmen were their elderly wives, dressed in their best and looking a little shy in the way of women who rarely go out. It was a moving sight. Old men remembering, divided by language but united by experience. Survivors, every one of them. We were glad to have witnessed it.

This endeared us to the *Auberge St Vincent*, and its other endearing quality was the price. The first few times we stayed there it was very inexpensive indeed. About £12 for a double room with one of those quaint washbasins and bidets that the French squash into impossible corners behind curtains. The lavatory was on the hallway outside. On our last visit we discovered that the owners had done even more miracles of squashing, managing to pack in a modern shower *and* a separate lavatory into a small bedroom. All of this had reduced the size of the room so that there was no way anyone of Falstaffian girth could possibly have got into either shower or lavatory in any comfort. But this bit of jigsaw-puzzling with the plumbing had enabled the hotel to double its prices at a stroke. Not that we were complaining. It was still a good £24 worth.

But the *Auberge St Vincent* is basically one of those hotels where one stays for the excellent food and not for the room. The owner/chef seems to have a bit of a sense of humour, as he bestows meaningless names on most of his dishes so that one doesn't know what one is getting. A starter is even called 'salad surprise' and I won't spoil the chef's fun by telling you what it is. However, if what one gets is a surprise, we've always found it to be a good one.

The Champagne region is, unfortunately, an area that people rush through when going South or returning home, because of its reasonable proximity to the coast. If, how-

ever, you can arrange your journey to have a few hours in
the area you won't have wasted your time. From the
autoroute there are no vineyards to be seen and it becomes
a puzzle as to where all that wonderful sparkling wine can
possibly come from in countryside that appears to grow
only wheat. Acres and acres of yellow wheat which, in the
early summer, is liberally sprinkled, Monet fashion, with
bright red poppies.

It's necessary to take to the by-ways to see the
vineyards and the uncompromising champagne villages
where the Champagnois live. If you leave the Reims by-
pass and take the Epernay road (the **N51**) you can pick up
the Route de Champagne. Stay on the **N51** for about
11km and then turn left into a village called
Villers-Allerand. This road skirts what is called the
Mountain of Reims – a high wooded area – where grapes
are grown on the slopes. The road has wonderful views of
orderly vineyards and is attractive at any time of year.
Even in the winter, when the vines look like nothing more
than a forest of gnarled, arthritic fingers, the black iron
stakes that support them make wonderful patterns, particularly against snow.

From here on, simply follow the Route de Champagne
signs and bowl along on empty roads through stern little
villages like **Rilly-la-Montagne**, **Chigny-les-Roses**, **Ludes**
and **Louvois**. Note the small placards at the side of the
vineyards which tell the passer-by for which of the great
champagne houses the grapes are being grown.

It is also worth driving the **N51** all the way to **Epernay**,
the second Champagne city after Reims. It is a road with
some spectacular views, where the scenery constantly
changes from enclosed woodlands to sweeping panoramas
of vineyards. The Marne runs through the town and they
do say that this is where the very best grapes of all are
grown.

Reims   Reims and Epernay have plenty of places to stay,
though it must be said that **Reims** is the more interesting
city, with its two wonderful Cathedrals and a very smart
shopping centre. There is even a Marks and Sparks,
though we find the food and wine shops more appealing.
This town suffered terribly in two World Wars, but it has
been rebuilt as a modern city. If you are interested in
what it looked like before, the shops sell postcards of old

68

Reims, mostly in a state of terrible destruction at the time of the First World War.

Epernay   **Epernay** is less interesting, except for its proximity to the Marne, but there you will find the grand Avenue de Champagne where some of the great marks, notably Moët et Chandon, have their headquarters.

A Taste of Bubbly

Many of the bigger champagne houses will give you a free guided tour of the premises and show you how the stuff is made – an experience that does leave one wondering why the product is so cheap! Such care and attention go into its creation. If you have time do take one of these tours. The most spectacular are those offered by Pommery et Greno in Reims and Moët et Chandon in Epernay: Pommery because their 32km of caves were originally dug by the Romans as chalk pits. These early invaders used the mined chalk blocks for building. In the huge chalk caverns deep underground there are some magnificent bas reliefs which wcre cut into the walls in the 1870s. Well worth seeing if you can cope with the walk down 116 steps into the caves (and the more demanding climb up again).

The Moët cellars are impressive for their very size. So big are they that the wine is moved over 29km on a small underground railway. There are something like 85 million bottles down there in various stages of manufacture. It would be easy to get lost without your guide – but what a lovely way to go.

Reims   When in **Reims** we normally stay at the *Hôtel de la Paix* on the Rue Buirette. Right in the centre of town and near the smart shopping area, it is basically a large, modern, commercial hotel with lots of leather furniture and a glossy bar. The rooms are comfortable, with televisions: modern and functional but well decorated. We like the hotel for its efficiency, though there are certainly cheaper and more picturesque places in Reims. The *de la Paix* has a garage; parking outside the hotel is comparatively simple if you don't want to pay the garage fee and they do not demand that you eat at the hotel, even though they have a large restaurant, *La Taverne de Maître Canter*. This is a brasserie-cum-beer-cellar, serving mostly Alsace-Lorraine specialities like sauerkraut and sausages. If you're in the mood and hungry it's good fun, with cheerful waiters, lots of carved wood and an alpine look, plus hearty portions. Frankly, almost impossibly hearty portions. Beer seems more popular than wine and comes in whopping great tankards. It is an ideal place to dine if you've missed lunch, are starving and not looking for *cordon bleu* cooking. Cost? Be prepared to part with up to £45 for the room, about £9 a head for the food. If you don't fancy Germanic cooking, Reims is full of good restaurants.

You will find *cordon bleu* cooking at *Le Florence*. This is a most elegant restaurant, quite small but with that air of bustle and professionalism that goes with a well run establishment. It also has a star for food, which makes *Le Florence* a treat, without being frighteningly expensive, though don't expect to get away with much under £35 a head with wine.

We discovered *Le Florence* when we were the guests of Philippe le Tuxerant, who has the extraordinary title of Délégué Extérieur d'Affaires du Comité Interprofessionnel du Vin de Champagne. We had a wonderful evening with superb food, though at first our host seemed a little preoccupied and asked if I would mind very much if he sat facing into the restaurant.

'Not at all,' I said, settling myself sidewards on to the room. He looked around the restaurant carefully. Then he sighed with satisfaction, beckoned the waiter and ordered a magnum of Mumm Champagne.

'Forgive me,' he said apologetically, 'but it was necessary to see who is in the restaurant before I ordered the wine. The directors of Mumm are at the table at the end of the room. They would have been deeply offended had I ordered another mark.'

Le Florence is a treat, and for the same reason it would be a sin to neglect to mention one very special hotel in Champagne – the *Royal Champagne*, at **Champillon**, near to Epernay. Unfortunately, staying and eating here costs an arm and a leg, but for a special occasion, it is well worth a visit. You will find it on the **N51**, between Reims and Epernay and near the village of Champillon. Look for

Champillon

it on the right going South. The hotel itself is small and
well kept, with a fine bar as you enter and, beyond, a
superb spacious dining room with a wonderful view across
vineyards and down to the Marne. It also serves excellent
food and the wine list boasts over 70 champagnes from
which to choose. Most of the bedrooms are in a separate
building outside, all elegantly furnished with doors leading
on to a garden.

We discovered the hotel when I was researching a
novel, *The Rose and the Vine*. The Comité
Interprofessionnel du Vin de Champagne – the body
which controls and promotes the wine – was being extremely helpful. Christian and Hélène Bizot, who own
Bollinger, had invited us to lunch and given us a tasting of
their finest wines – something which turned out to be
what you might call an historical event. It was in the early
1900s when Champagne lost all its vines to a nasty little
aphid called *phylloxera*, that chewed equally happily on
the roots or the leaves of the vines. Either way, it killed
them.

The cure came when it was discovered that wild vine
stock, indigenous to the United States, would resist the
phylloxera. All French (indeed, all European) vine stocks
were gradually grafted onto American roots and, fortunately for all of us who love the grape, the wine industry was
saved.

Today Bollinger grow the only pre-*phylloxera* vines left
in Champagne. In Ay they retain a walled vineyard, where
the grapes still come from the old stock and a small quan-
tity of wine is made from them.

There are those who say that wine made from vines
with the American roots is not as good as it was pre-
phylloxera. We drank wine made from these original vines
with Monsieur Bizot, who, incidentally, is the nephew of
the late Madame Bollinger. It was definitely an experience, but, alas, I could not tell any difference. But then I
am no expert.

The highlight of this particular research trip was when
we met Colonel François Bonal from the CIVC. He took
us to dinner at the *Royal Champagne*. A retired soldier, a
connoisseur of champagne and an expert on its growth and
manufacture, he had agreed to talk to us about his favourite subject.

He arrived, an elderly, elegant man, tall, straight-backed, and very much the soldier. We met him in the bar of the hotel and he sat himself down in his good tweed suit and ordered a bottle of the house champagne, explaining in perfect English that one should start with the house wine, which was very drinkable and excellent value, before one went on to something more serious.

We polished off that bottle before going into dine and the 'something more serious' turned out to be three more bottles of vintage champagne, one Pol Roger to go with the hors d'oeuvres, one Krug to go with the main course, and a bottle of Moët *douce* to go with the pudding. I fear we never left a drop. Nor did we refuse the Marc de Champagne that came with the coffee.

Apart from this profusion of the best, the Colonel was an excellent raconteur, full of stories concerning what was obviously a grand passion. One fact that stuck in my mind through this haze of good living was that the CIVC now actually fixes a date when the *vignerons* may begin picking their grapes. This is to prevent the growers from picking too soon in an attempt to get ahead of their competitors. They can wait longer if they wish and if they feel their grapes are not ready, but they must not begin picking earlier than the chosen date. There is one exception to this rule. It applies to the vineyards around Hautvillers, where the monk Dom Perignon first discovered how to make champagne. On this hillside the grapes ripen earlier, and the Hautvillers *vignerons* are permitted to pick two days before everyone else.

I went to bed that night fearful of the most terrible hangover. But not a bit of it. I woke feeling wonderful. Which says a lot for vintage champagne.

3

From Calais to Paris

Having taken a rambling journey to and from the South, let us now proceed in an orderly fashion along each section of the autoroutes and roads which lead from the North of France to the Mediterranean.

Since most British people who travel to France embark and disembark at the Kent channel ports, we'll make our start from Dover or Folkestone on either ferry or Sea-cat before covering other ports.

From Dover or Folkestone it makes sense to head for **Calais**, where the **A26** autoroute that begins the journey South commences. The **A26** starts just 6km from the Calais port at the end of a well signposted drive through the town. This autoroute will eventually link up with the Channel Tunnel when, no doubt, it will become more crowded than it is now. For the moment it is singularly under-used and leads to the much busier **A1**, which takes traffic through Northern France and to the Paris Périphérique.

You can also land in France with the Sally Line from Ramsgate at **Dunkerque** where the **A25** autoroute begins about 13km out of town. This goes to the big industrial city of Lille, swings under the town and joins up with the autoroute you *really* want at Arras. If you do land at Dunkerque it is possible to save some mileage by cutting across country and picking up the **A26** at Béthune. The route is described on page 177.

Unfortunately you have to go through the centre of Béthune to pick up the **A26** which is why we really don't advise starting from Dunkerque. It is not particularly

73

interesting countryside and is all a bit of a performance. Generally speaking, unless you have some very good reason for starting from Dunkerque – like the crossing being cheaper, especially if you are willing to leave at 11pm – it is not worth it. You arrive in a rather dreary town that is also further North and not really the direction you want to go. Added to which, the sea crossing takes $2\frac{1}{2}$ hours, as against the 75 minutes from Dover to Calais on a P & O super-ferry. Even an ordinary ferry takes only 90 minutes.

Boulogne The other alternative is to disembark at **Boulogne**, which is a much more interesting little town than Dunkerque. Here you are deposited a few miles further South on your journey. The bad news is that the crossing takes roughly 20 minutes longer than to Calais and there is about 52km of country driving to get you back on the right track at **St Omer**. It's a simple journey. Out of Boulogne, follow the signposts for St Omer and stay on the **N42** until you reach the blue autoroute signs. This is a pleasant drive, but not *that* pleasant, and it is not worth lingering at this stage of the game unless you have plenty of time. Calais makes a more practical jumping-off point.

If you do decide on **Boulogne**, you'll eat well. The town has a good selection of restaurants. If we are feeling flush we like the *La Liégeoise* in the Rue A Monsigny. At about £22 a head with wine, it is an elegant restaurant serving carefully prepared and presented food. We've been known to get on the boat on a Sunday just to have lunch there.

After the disaster when the *Métropole* hotel locked me out, we now stay at the simpler *Faidherbe*, run by Madame Dollans. This has very small but cosy rooms and a dear little sitting room with a log fire downstairs, off the lobby, where lives a parrot called Victor. Madame Dollans insists that Victor is learning to speak English and getting on well. It's a pleasant spot to sit quietly for a while and chat to Victor. The hotel is near the front, is a touch quaint, has no restaurant and costs around £30 for a double with bath, £25 with shower. All rooms have a TV and, this near to Britain, you can sometimes pick up *Neighbours*, should you want to.

This is quite pricey for this class of hotel in France, but Boulogne, being such a tourist attraction, can get away

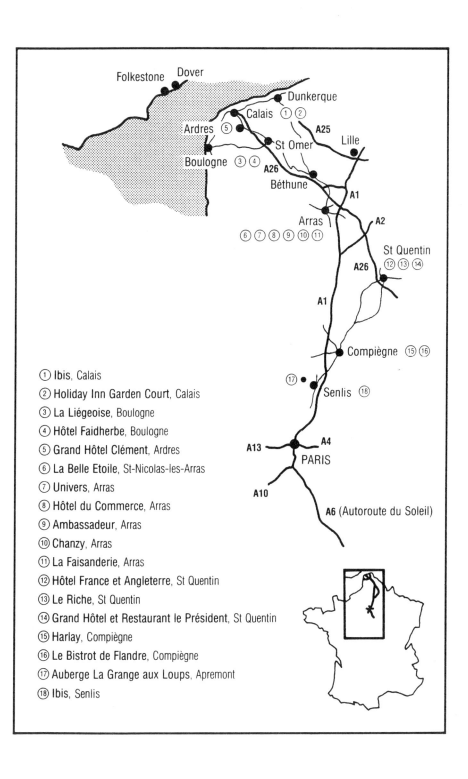

Folkestone Dover

Dunkerque

Calais ① ②

Ardres ⑤

A25

St Omer Lille

Boulogne ③ ④

A26

Béthune

A1

Arras A2

⑥ ⑦ ⑧ ⑨ ⑩ ⑪

St Quentin

A26 ⑫ ⑬ ⑭

A1

Compiègne ⑮ ⑯

⑰

Senlis ⑱

A13 A4

PARIS

A10

A6 (Autoroute du Soleil)

① Ibis, Calais
② Holiday Inn Garden Court, Calais
③ La Liégeoise, Boulogne
④ Hôtel Faidherbe, Boulogne
⑤ Grand Hôtel Clément, Ardres
⑥ La Belle Etoile, St-Nicolas-les-Arras
⑦ Univers, Arras
⑧ Hôtel du Commerce, Arras
⑨ Ambassadeur, Arras
⑩ Chanzy, Arras
⑪ La Faisanderie, Arras
⑫ Hôtel France et Angleterre, St Quentin
⑬ Le Riche, St Quentin
⑭ Grand Hôtel et Restaurant le Président, St Quentin
⑮ Harlay, Compiègne
⑯ Le Bistrot de Flandre, Compiègne
⑰ Auberge La Grange aux Loups, Apremont
⑱ Ibis, Senlis

with charging more. And one can always economise by eating a great hearty meal along with the town's fishermen at the *Hamiot* opposite. This restaurant is more of a bustling café, with something going on all the time. The food, particularly the fish, is great in a hearty, chips-with-everything way, and will barely dent your pocket.

Do consider taking an evening ferry if it is possible on your schedule (there are sailings from Dover all through the night) and sleeping either in or near Calais or Boulogne. This is both cheaper and pleasanter than stopping in Dover. The ferry can cost less at night and hotel rooms in France are considerably less costly – and you'll most certainly get a better supper. It's madness to stay in the expensive gastronomic desert that is Dover. And in the morning you will be fresh for your drive through France.

Calais
Calais is awash with simple hotels, and if you are arriving very late and wanting to start early it is probably wiser to stay at one of the sensibly priced chain hotels, such as the *Ibis*, where there is a night porter to let you in should the boat be late. All rooms have bath or shower, TV and cost £30 the night. The well signposted hotel is also situated on the way to the autoroute, so that you can set off good and early in the morning. It is surrounded by other inexpensive hotels, so there should be no problem about finding accommodation.

If you get to Calais early enough to have a look round, do stay by the port, which is charming and full of life, with masses of cafés and restaurants. We usually visit the *Café de Paris* at the top of the smart Rue Royale and near the Place d'Armes. They serve excellent coffee, though, this being France, you can have a drink if that's what you fancy. Most importantly, they have a nice clean loo! It's surprising how many quite smart-seeming establishments in France still offer their customers a hole in the ground and a chain that flushes water all over your shoes! I have learned to pull and leap backwards at the same time. Since men are better constructed for this primitive form of sanitation, it is Phil's job to inspect the plumbing, usually quickly and furtively so that we can slip out without ordering if there aren't proper facilities.

This port area of Calais is very attractive, with a lighthouse and some interesting Dutch-style modern buildings, and you can watch the ferries come and go. The *Holiday Inn Garden Court* overlooks the water and there are plenty of small, simple hotels to choose from. The town is extremely well signposted, so you won't have any trouble getting yourself to the autoroute after your stay. In the days when I was working full-time, I would sneak off early on the Friday, drive to Dover and cross the channel at the first opportunity, as I preferred to get a little out of Calais ready for the next morning.

Ardres   The pleasant little town of **Ardres** is only 17km out of Calais, and it is well placed for picking up the autoroute the next morning. Though small, Ardres is well served for hotels and restaurants. Our favourite is the dignified *Grand Hôtel Clément*, white-fronted and with an imposing gable, on the Esplanade Maréchal Leclerc. It is one of those faintly faded, old-fashioned hotels that you feel will never change, but it has a star for food and is well-known to the travelling cognoscenti. Therefore, if you wish to stay at the *Clément*, it is wise to book, as they only have 17 rooms. But expect a sizeable bill. The rooms are inexpensive; the food is not. No restaurant in France with Michelin stars is ever cheap.

Another point about Ardres is that, if you should be returning to Britain on a Sunday, you can catch the town's weekly Sunday morning market. We like to make a point of stopping to buy a supper of French bread, tomatoes, pâté and some of those delicious ready-made dishes from the *traiteur* before we catch the boat back. Coming home to a French repast softens the blow of leaving. You can, incidentally, take any kind of cooked meat as long as it is packaged, bread, pastries, fruit and vegetables or even raw fish into Britain without getting into trouble with the customs. Only raw meat is banned.

Arras   If you can manage to get even further on the way than Ardres, **Arras** is an ideal place to stop. It takes exactly an hour to drive there on the autoroute from Calais and has a great many pleasant little hotels to choose from. The only snag is that, if your car is temptingly laden, only two of the town's hotels, *La Belle Etoile*, a motel-type establishment, and the *Univers*, the most expensive hotel in town, have parking.

The *Belle Etoile* is recommended only if you arrive too late for a stroll and an exploration, and want to get off at the crack of dawn. It is not close to the town centre – rather more in the slightly industrial area of St Nicolas, though it does have quite a pretty view. It also has the virtue of being close to the **N17**, the road that leads to the autoroute. The rooms there are basic and well organised, with television and the usual beige/brown plastic of a modern stopping place: functional. The food is good and hearty – they serve one of those help-yourself-eat-as-much-as-you-like hors d'oeuvres as a starter and there is certainly nothing to complain about, except its location. The price is definitely reasonable, with rooms under £30 for a double with bath and the cheapest menu at about £7.50.

Personally, though, we prefer to stay in the town, particularly as Arras has a couple of spectacular squares in the Dutch style and some fine ancient buildings. If you're only looking for an inexpensive place to stay, the *Hôtel du Commerce* on the Rue Gambetta, near the station, has no restaurant but is clean, decent and inexpensive (between £12 and £23). Of course, for £12 you do not get a shower or a lavatory. Out of 40 rooms, 20 have a shower. It has no garage and once when staying there my car was broken into and my suitcases and those of the woman I was travelling with were taken. Of course I was insured (as I am sure you will be, too) but the inconvenience is considerable. By the time the window was mended and the police had taken details and given me a paper for the insurance company it was well gone midday before we were on our way again.

There were two lessons to be learned from this. Never travel without adequate insurance and never leave too much visible in the car. If you have to leave the car in the street get as much as possible in the boot and take what is left into the hotel. It's also important to know that if you do have an accident, are robbed or lose something, should you be claiming insurance it is essential to report the incident to the French police, who will give you the correct documents for your insurance company. You need the *gendarmerie* for anything to do with traffic and your car; the police for theft or loss. The *gendarmerie* are not particularly sympathetic about small bumps and dents in motor cars, as a friend of ours who reported a collision in Paris can testify.

'Is anyone dead?' asked the gendarme.

On being assured that there was no loss of life, he asked: 'Then why are you bothering me?' and turned his attention to something more urgent.

For all these reasons it does make sense to put your car either in a garage or a private parking, if you can't get everything securely locked in the boot. But you will be charged a few francs extra, certainly if it is a lock-up garage.

Apart from this lack of a garage, the *Commerce* is an adequate stopping place when hard-up. There was a time when it was even more basic and incredibly cheap. In recent years the hotel has been improved and it seems they now get a better class of client. Gone from above the bedroom bidets are the desperate, angrily scrawled signs which stated: HERE IS NOT TOILET!

If you have time to stop for a while you will find Arras is a most attractive town. Spending time as we do on the Kent coast, we often take friends there for lunch and play a little game. Our guests are told that lunch will be unpretentious and that we are going to the Arras station buffet. The reaction is always the same. A flicker of dismay, followed by assurances that anywhere will do, and that it will certainly be an experience.

In fact, the station buffet is roughly where we are going, except that the *Ambassadeur*, as the station restaurant is called, is elegant with fresh flowers, formal waiters, fine linen and silver, serving excellent food at about £15 a head. It has large windows, discreetly netted for privacy, which look out over the square, chandeliers, classic furniture and is close-carpeted for calm. It is, in fact, something of an experience as a station restaurant. They are particularly good at duck, and all their meat and poultry is specially raised for the owner, Alain Souffront, on a nearby farm. The salmon is also smoked locally. Our guests find it a pleasant surprise.

Less expensive is the *Chanzy*, a cheerful little hotel/restaurant on the Rue Chanzy just off the station square, but most of the British who stop at Arras seem to land up at the *Univers*. This is a splendid, slightly-gone-to-seed grand hotel in a most elegant long-windowed building which began its existence as a 16th-century monastery. It is set in a quiet square, the Place Croix-Rouge, and the rooms are all placed around a central courtyard, where there is a pretty

garden hidden behind stone arches. It is blessedly quiet
considering it is right bang in the middle of town. We like
the *Univers*. It has jolly good bathrooms and comfortable
beds in big, faded, plushy rooms that cost around £30 for
the night. Some have four-poster beds. We don't know
whether to blame our fellow-countrymen for the fact that
the food could be a great deal better, though the charm
and distinction of Monsieur Gilleron, the *directeur* of the
elegantly appointed restaurant, make all forgivable.

Monsieur Gilleron once astounded us by shaking his
head gently when Philip had ordered a rather good bottle
of wine.

'You are certain?' he asked. 'Since Madame is having
fish with fruit –' skate with raspberries to be exact, which
was not a great success – 'and you are having an omelette,
perhaps a Chablis would be more suitable.'

The Chablis was half the price.

A night at the *Univers*, if you eat there, will cost around
£80, but the rooms really are not expensive for what you
get, and it is not a house rule that you must take dinner
there, as in many French hotels. So you can always pop
down to the *Chanzy* for supper or, if money is no object,
visit the lovely *Faisanderie* in the Grand-Place.

This restaurant is a class act from the moment you set
foot in the charming lobby and are gently led downstairs
into the restaurant itself. Though the setting is a 15th-
century *cave*, there is no sense of being underground. The
room is cleverly lit and cosy, with warm red-brick walls
and ceiling and arches supported by stone pillars. It is one
of those restaurants where some of the goodies are on
display, getting the taste buds going. The food is basically
nouvelle cuisine, but the portions are not ungenerous. As
this restaurant has a well-deserved Michelin star, you can
expect to pay at least £25 a head with wine.

The courtesy at the *Faisanderie* takes some beating. We
once arrived there for lunch, thinking it was 1.30pm and
not knowing we had got ourselves in some time warp. The
head-waiter looked discreetly at his watch and murmured
that if we were prepared to go down right away they
would be delighted to serve us.

It wasn't until we were drinking our coffee in an empty
restaurant that we found we had actually arrived at
2.30pm. And still no-one seemed anxious for us to leave.

St Quentin

If you have time to press on even further, a good stopping place is **St Quentin**, as it is cosily tucked by the autoroute. It would not be true to say that this is a fascinating town, though it is quite lively and there are tasteful and elegant dress and shoe shops and some interesting Flemish architecture. The trouble is that they seem to have been tearing out the centre square to create an underground car-park for ever. This work must finish one day (it was getting close in the summer of 1991) and then the beautiful old square and the Basilique which stands nearby will come back into their own.

But it can be a handy stopping place, and we usually stay at the *France et Angleterre* hotel for the same boring reason that it has a lock-up garage and is right in the centre of the town, near to the Basilique. The hotel could not be more ordinary. The bedrooms are truly basic, with those funny suction pump-action loos which make a most embarrassing noise when you flush them. But the young couple, Monsieur and Madame Brunet, who run the place, are so pleasant and eager to please that I forgave every bang I had on the shins from the oddly shaped bed in our small room. Also, the hotel has no restaurant, which gives time to explore and anyway, how can you expect great décor from an establishment that only charges about £20 a night for a double room with shower?

In St Quentin we wandered off and found ourselves a pleasant restaurant for dinner. Set in the middle of the pedestrian precinct of the Rue des Toiles, off the main square, *Le Riche* is wide open to the pavement: a big, high-ceilinged café, lots of mirrors, bustle and noise. The waiters were of the seen-it-all, done-it-all variety and with the brusque efficiency of Northern France. Monsieur Slamant, the proprietor, and his family have owned the restaurant since 1930 and it has a good atmosphere.

Phil ate his favourite *escargots* followed by an omelette. I had a tray of whelks, winkles, cockles, shrimps and prawns, followed by steak and chips. French chips, all thin, small, crisp and delicious. With a bottle of house wine, the bill was knocking £25. Not bad, and anyway, it is one of those very French restaurants where the atmosphere is all. Had we stuck to the menu we could have eaten for under £8, or gone mad and had the most expensive menu at £20 a head.

If you fancy somewhere rather more exotic, down near the old port (St Quentin has an important canal) to the South of the town is the *Grand Hôtel* and its accompanying *Le Président* restaurant. Both are really rather special. The hotel was renovated in 1988 and with great taste. There is a glass lift that rises in an open atrium, where passengers to the three floors of the hotel can look down on a charming reception area and a pretty little indoor terrace set about with garden furniture. The bedrooms are smart, with mini-bar, television and a sitting area. The bathrooms are most definitely all mod-cons. The price, under £50, does not seem unreasonable.

But the restaurant, another with one Michelin star, is an experience. It is set in quite a small but very pretty room. The Empire chairs are upholstered in rose chintz, the pink tablecloths have green and cream striped undercloths. A small bowl of roses is placed on every table, and the atmosphere is light, bright and sophisticated. The food, cooked by Jean-Marc Le Guennec, is truly wonderful and good value for money.

While waiting for our first course, we were served two different *bonnes bouches*, small pieces of stuffed pasta. The menu was under £20, service included, and for our first course we were presented with what looked not unlike a fish-cake, made of skate. The fish was cold, but surrounded by tiny little hot spring vegetables and a piquant sauce made, I suspect, with a touch of ginger. It was delicious and there was a lot of it. Quite enough for a full course. The main course consisted of thinly sliced veal kidney with a few tiny golden potato cakes along with delicate little vegetables, including bean shoots and flavoured with soy sauce. No cheese, but a beautifully prepared and presented raspberry mousse on a biscuit crust. With a plateful of *petits fours* and some excellent coffee, we were in urgent need of a walk before bed. Our bill for the night was £130 – quite a leap from the £60 odd pounds we spent at the *France et Angleterre* and *Le Riche*. But we felt it was worth it.

St Quentin is just slightly to the West of Paris on the way to Reims, beyond Arras, but at Arras comes decision time: whether to take the **A1** to Paris or go off to the East on the **A26** through Reims and down to Dijon.

Since we have already covered the **A26** in our **Autumn**

Journey, let us now veer off onto the **A1** and Paris.

Should the timing of your crossing have left you needing to stay the night nearer to Paris than Arras, the best stopping place is **Compiègne**, just 80km from the capital. It is an interesting and historical town. The Summer Palace of the Kings of France is there and gets a couple of stars in the Michelin guide, meaning that it is worth a detour to visit. There is also the *Clairière de L'Armistice* – the clearing in the woods where the Armistice ending the First World War was signed. This is just outside the town and if you have time you can see the railway carriage in which the peace document was signed.

The river Oise flows through the centre of Compiègne, spanned by a rather fine bridge, and the town is a well kept, reasonably prosperous, typical Northern French town.

But where to stay? After my desperate, but eventually perfectly acceptable, night in the *Palais des Sports* there, we went to the other extreme and stayed at the rather more upmarket *Harlay*. This hotel is set romantically on the Quai with rooms overlooking the river and an attractive double with bath and wc costs around £30 for the night. Monsieur and Madame Boco are fourth-generation owners of the *Harlay* and they have been making improvements gradually over the last couple of years. There is no restaurant, though the breakfast room, with its view of the river, is charming. For meals, Madame Boco points guests in the direction of the *Bistrot de Flandre* round the corner, on the Rue d'Amiens, a recommendation which has not yet received a complaint, since you will eat there very well for about £9 a head, without wine. Their speciality is steak. The *Harlay* has a huge parking space for guests behind the hotel and because of this it is one of the few hotels where you ask for a room at the front if you want some peace and quiet. At the back you can be woken early by the coming and going of cars and deliveries.

Even nearer to Paris – only 50km – is the nice little town of **Senlis**. Senlis has an *Ibis Hotel* most sensibly placed just a few kilometres off the autoroute on the **RN324**. Since the earlier you get yourself through Paris the simpler the journey is, this no-frills but totally reliable chain hotel is a good place to stop, as you can be on your way without delay.

We have friends who can't manage to get a boat much before lunchtime and Senlis is their stopping point. They find that by leaving the *Ibis* at about 6am they miss the worst of the rush hour on the Paris Périphérique. If, however, you are travelling on a Sunday morning, unless there is racing at either Longchamps or Le Mans, it is not necessary to rise so early. On Sunday mornings the Périphérique is comparatively peaceful.

You can, of course, eat at *Ibis* Hotels, but since it's not obligatory, our friends prefer to go to a restaurant and there is a charming one, the *Auberge La Grange aux*

Apremont *Loups*, in the tiny village of **Apremont**, where our friends head once they have settled in at the *Ibis*. The wife suspects that her husband likes to go there because the waitresses are remarkably pretty! Both agree, however, that it is a restaurant with a touch of class, well run by a sophisticated proprietor, with a smart clientele all in an old-world setting. Lots of beams, big open fire, natural stone walls and a refined cuisine of dishes such as a beautifully presented salmon *en croûte*.

To get there from the *Ibis* you turn on to the **N330**, direction Creil. This is a ring road around Senlis and becomes the dual carriageway **RN16**. Watch for the signpost to Apremont on your right, since you will have to swing back under the dual carriageway. The restaurant is in the Rue du 11 Novembre, but you won't have any trouble finding it in this small village.

From Senlis, the **A1** runs straight to the Périphérique at the **Porte de la Chapelle**. Don't let yourself be deflected earlier. There are two other autoroutes which run off the **A1** – the **A104** and the **A3** – which you will see signposted not long after you have had the surprising experience of driving under the runways of Charles de Gaulle airport.

You are unlikely to be tempted by the **A104**, since it is signposted Metz, but if you do get yourself on to the **A3**, which goes round the East of Paris, panic not. It will bring you back on to the Périphérique, but further round, at the **Porte de Bagnolet**.

Once at Porte de la Chapelle, swing left on to the Périphérique – always keeping to Paris Est. The direction to follow is **Porte d'Aubervilliers**, the next exit on this ring road. Navigation round the Périphérique is not difficult as long as you know which *porte* you are aiming for.

To pick up the **Autoroute du Soleil** you need to get to the **Porte d'Italie**. (If by chance you have got yourself to the Porte de Bagnolet, all the same rules apply.) Turn left, keep to Paris Est and look for Porte d'Italie, though from Bagnolet you will first be directed to the Porte de Montreuil.

From la Chapelle, Porte d'Italie is the 15th *porte* in the ring. Best to do this road quietly and gently, as it is four lanes wide, containing a mixture of tunnels and bridges, all ruthlessly carved round the edge of the city and which allow tantalising views of the Sacré-Coeur and Eiffel Tower. Site yourself in the second or third lane, don't let yourself be harassed and plod gently on, ticking off the *portes* as you pass them. This is no place for dashing about in the fast lane.

The *portes* come in this order:

de la Chapelle
d'Aubervilliers
de la Villette
de Pantin
du Pré-St Gervais
des Lilas
de Bagnolet
de Montreuil
de Vincennes
de St Mandé
Dorée
de Charenton
de Bercy
Quai d'Ivry
Porte d'Ivry
d'Italie

In order to avoid last minute panics, at **Quai d'Ivry**, get yourself into the second lane, and move into the slow lane before **Porte d'Ivry** so that you are well placed to slide off at Porte d'Italie. You will find that the road is very well signposted to the **Autoroute du Soleil** (which is officially the **A6** at this point.) Just follow **A6** and **Autoroute du Soleil** signs and it's a piece of cake. You are on your way South.

If you by any chance miss the exit at Porte d'Italie you can still join the **A6** by leaving the Périphérique at the next exit, the Porte de Gentilly.

Coming North, reverse the procedure: stick to the Paris Est and Porte d'Italie signs. Slide off the autoroute at Porte d'Italie and swing on to the Périphérique, direction Porte d'Ivry, and keep going until you reach la Chapelle. There you are directed on to the **A1**. Don't forget to get yourself into the slow lane at Porte d'Aubervilliers ready to slide off.

Never go West of Paris when using the Périphérique unless you are travelling to or from Le Havre or Caen. In theory, it shouldn't matter if you do go the wrong way, since as you are going round a circle you must eventually land up where you want to be. But going West takes longer. Also, one of the *portes* which leads to the Normandy autoroute is called Boulogne Billancourt. The number of British who mistake this for the road to Boulogne must be legion. They come off the Périphérique with a great sigh of relief – on to the wrong autoroute and speed off in the direction of Le Havre. The penny drops too late and they have a long cross-country drive to get to their boat (usually missed) at Calais or Boulogne proper.

Some people go to great lengths to avoid the Périphérique, but it really is not terrifying as long as you take it steady and avoid the fast lanes, where the French do jockey for position. Of course, you could make Paris your stopping point, but unless you have plenty of time this is not a good idea. Paris, with its many one-way streets, is an easy place in which to get lost unless you know it well. Much better to visit Paris on a different occasion without a car. If you must stop there, ask your travel agent to find you an hotel close to one of the *portes* so that at least you can get in and out easily, but remember that the *portes* are not in the parts of Paris that you probably would like to see. Far better to take a weekend there as a separate holiday.

When coming from Calais, the only really sensible way to avoid Paris without a lot of cross-country driving is to go around Reims. Otherwise you can do complicated things such as swinging to the East from **Senlis** and driving down the **N330** to **Meaux**. Outside Meaux pick up the **A4** autoroute for a short distance before coming off at the exit for **Melun**, where you take the **N36** to Melun. In this town follow the blue signs for the autoroute, **Nemours** and **Auxerre**.

Sounds simple, and on the map it looks quite simple, but it is a pain to drive. You have to edge your way through the busy towns of Meaux and Melun and the roads are not all dual carriageway, and are very busy.

When driving to the Côte d'Azur, you are, of course, driving North to South, but you are also constantly bearing East. Nice, Antibes and Cannes are well to the South-east and no distance from Italy. Therefore, if you stay West at the beginning of your journey, the further you travel, the longer the West-to-East journey you have to make to pick up the autoroutes to the South. If you haven't time to wander, it makes sense to set off in an Easterly direction. And even if you've time for a little dalliance, East still makes more sense.

To the West there is no clear, direct way round Paris. If you want to stay to the West, perhaps to see the wonderful Cathedrals of Rouen or Chartres, there is little point in bothering with the autoroute from Calais. The thing to do is to drive through the countryside (route on page 177), abandoning all thoughts of moving quickly. Having reached **Chartres** it is possible to leave by autoroute **A11**, and by travelling slightly to the North-east, pick up the **A6** just outside Paris at **Chilly Mazarin**. This Calais-Chartres-A6 route is described on page 177 for those who feel more comfortable on a direct road than threading their way through the country.

Personally, we find it irritating to go backwards, and a much more rewarding and considerably shorter road which shows you the charming little town of **Milly-le-Fôret** is described on page 178.

But what about those who are leaving Britain from other ports than Dover or Folkestone? Read on . . .

4

Going South from Caen, Le Havre or Dieppe

From a distance and convenience point of view, the very best place to arrive in France when going South is undoubtedly Le Havre. The worst, unless you are heading for the South-west and Spain, is Roscoff. The second worst, Cherbourg. These ports, along with St Malo, are like the old story of the traveller lost in Ireland who, when he asks for directions, is told, 'I wouldn't start from here if I were you.' And neither would I.

Le Havre

Le Havre is a great place to begin. It is about 180km South of Calais and the Autoroute de Normandie (**A13**), which goes direct to Paris, begins only 48km from the town. (The **A15** autoroute leading to it starts as you leave Le Havre.) The **A13** runs into the Périphérique at Boulogne Billancourt where, to get to the Autoroute du Soleil, you swing right, direction Porte d'Auteuil and Porte St Cloud.

Going round the Périphérique, pass Porte de Versailles and Porte de Chatillon. Next comes Porte d'Orléans. Ease into the slow lane ready to come off on to the well marked **A6** – the Autoroute du Soleil.

If conditions on the Périphérique are kind, it is possible to be round and out of Paris two hours after leaving Le Havre. The snag is that the sailings to this port on the Seine are slow. There are two P & O daytime crossings

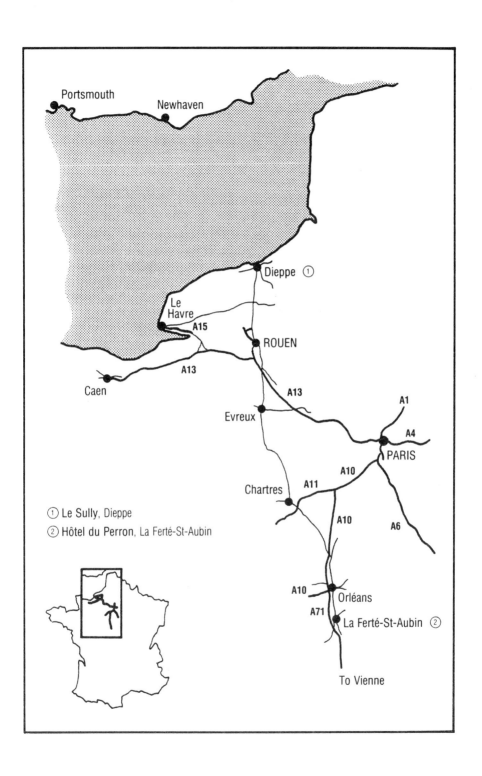

Portsmouth

Newhaven

Dieppe ①

Le
Havre
A15

ROUEN

A13

Caen

A13

Evreux

A1

A4

PARIS

A10

Chartres **A11**

① Le Sully, Dieppe
② Hôtel du Perron, La Ferté-St-Aubin

A10

A6

A10

Orléans

A71

La Ferté-St-Aubin ②

To Vienne

from Portsmouth to Le Havre in season, and they take 5¾ hours. The more practical, the morning crossing, leaves at 8.30am and docks at 3.15pm French time, leaving time to reach the other side of Paris. The night crossing leaves Portsmouth at 11pm and takes 7 hours (8 hours coming back). It arrives at 7am, allowing for the hour's time difference, and gives you an early start to your driving day. Unfortunately, unless you are prepared to pay for a berth, which costs around £12, the night-time crossing can sometimes be not much fun. The problem is that one can't legislate against hordes of school-kids and drunks galloping round the ship all night. It is possible to hire a reclining seat with rug thrown in for under £4 in a particular lounge which is supposed to be a silent rest area. But school-kids and drunks are no respecters of people who are trying to sleep. Club class is one answer at £8, again with rug, but in a more private area.

If you want a berth, book early: they are in short supply. This night crossing from Portsmouth to Le Havre is a good one, but only if you have slept the night and are not starting the day exhausted. If you have been awake most of the night and start driving at 7am when the boat docks, obviously it can be dangerous. We have a young friend who wrecked his and his friend's holiday by falling asleep at the wheel at 10am after sitting up all night on a ferry. Though all four in the car saw the inside of a French hospital, fortunately no-one was seriously hurt. But bouncing off the crash barrier didn't do the car much good. If you don't have a berth, travel with at least two drivers; and no-one should *ever* drive when tired.

Caen   An alternative is to land in **Caen** from Portsmouth if the boat times suit you better. Though Caen looks as if it is further from Paris, there isn't much in it: a matter of about 50km more driving, though you can shorten this a little by avoiding the autoroute. Another possibility, depending on the boat times that suit your schedule, is

Dieppe   Newhaven-**Dieppe**, where there is about 40km of driving before you pick up the **A15** into Rouen. Dieppe is the nearest and by far the most interesting of these three Normandy towns to Paris, but the problem with Dieppe is getting round Rouen to pick up the Autoroute de Normandie. Explanations for directions from Caen and Dieppe are on pages 178 and 179.

Don't forget that these are all long sea-crossings which cut into your time unless you can travel overnight.

There was a time when we nearly always crossed Portsmouth-Le Havre at night. We no longer do so as we have a cottage in Kent, only eight miles from Dover. But I liked the 7am start and reaching Paris so quickly. With a passenger who had never seen the glory of Chartres Cathedral, we would skirt Paris so that they could see this great edifice dominating the skyline and stop for a while to enjoy the intense blue of the windows. One reaches here just about the right time for a cup of coffee and, having refreshed ourselves spiritually and physically, we would pick up the Autoroute du Soleil by the route suggested on page 178.

Either going direct into Paris or cutting through the countryside if starting from Le Havre at 7am, the result is the same. If you don't linger too long over lunch you will be looking for a night's accommodation the other side of Lyon with the worst of the journey over.

Equally, it is possible to keep West all the way down to **St Etienne** in the South, avoiding Paris and its outskirts. One leaves the Normandy autoroute at **Evreux** for **Chartres**. From Chartres head for **Orléans** and as there is autoroute all the way from there to **Vienne** you will still end the day's journey the other side of Lyon. The bonus is that you drive through the beautiful Midi countryside, and the further South you go, the more mountainous and dramatic the scenery becomes. The route is described on page 181. This is an interesting drive if you have the time. Starting from Calais it is tediously long. Starting from Le Havre, Dieppe or Caen it is a reasonable way to go.

La Ferté-St-Aubin

One stopping place on this route which fits in very neatly on the journey when coming North is the *Hôtel du Perron* in the small town of **La Ferté-St-Aubin**, 13km South of Orléans on the **N20**. One leaves the autoroute at Orléans Sud to get to it. This is one of Dick and Kath's discoveries, made when they were having difficulty in tracking down an hotel. They had got themselves lost in the countryside outside Orléans when they saw a sign in the middle of nowhere giving directions to a golf-club. Hopeful that it might just have accommodation, they de-cided to give it a try. They found no bed, but they did find a suave, laid-back Welshman who was the owner of

91

the club. He recommended them to the *Hôtel du Perron*, and even telephoned to book them a room. They were warmly greeted by an English-speaking receptionist who showed them to their room. It proved to be typical of its class, but at under £25 for a double it did have a shower and a wc. (Over £30 with bath.)

Now our Dickie is generously built, in rotund fashion. Having stripped off to shower after a long day's driving, he came up against a snag. He couldn't get into the shower. The sliding doors were narrower than he was. He suggested that Kath give him an almighty shove to get him in. She simply wasn't having it, pointing out the embarrassment if she had to call for help to get him out again.

He would have had the same problem in our favourite *Auberge St Vincent* in Ambonnay, and in many other small hotels. This is all down to the French determination to upgrade their rooms by putting in private wcs and at the least a shower. In small rooms this requires a miracle of juggling space. But however quaint or tiny the result, it's a million times better than begging for the bathroom key as one still has to do in so many British hotels.

Dickie, washed but not showered, went down to dinner muttering that Bernard Jaquet, President of the France Accueil group, which owns the Perron, should be told that at least one of his shower doors needs widening. Unless, of course, he added, the intention is that their hotels should only be patronised by thin people.

An excellent meal proved soothing. The dining room was steeped in atmosphere, all beams and timbers, and the bill about £13 a head for the cheapest menu. Michel Darchis, the chef/patron at the *Perron*, specialises in game, which in France is never hung for as long as in Britain. Therefore, if you normally find a pheasant or a partridge too high and too aromatic by far, you might just find that in France you enjoy it.

Dieppe

From La Ferté-St-Aubin it is a comfortable ride back to the Normandy ports. If you are fortunate enough to hit **Dieppe** on a Saturday you will catch the market. This is a bit special, for several reasons. Fruits and vegetables on sale there are remarkably cheap. This is the port where much of the imported food arrives, and bunches of bananas or exotic fruits that are just too ripe to travel further find their way on to the market stalls. Farmers' wives come in from the Normandy countryside and set up a table to display their own cheeses, eggs and butter. At the fish-market here you can buy the best raw scallops and mussels you have ever tasted, and it's permitted to bring all of it home.

Round off the experience by having lunch at the *Sully* – a delightful small restaurant right on the quay, almost up against the big ships that berth in Dieppe. The food at the *Sully* is hearty – wonderful rabbit dishes, and, not surprisingly, excellent fish. You can choose between a £6, £9 and £11 menu, so it is not expensive by any means. But it is the atmosphere that is so attractive. As you enter the door you are greeted by the sound of singing birds. Lots of birds in a huge cage, darting, flying, cheeping and seemingly perfectly happy. Admittedly it's hard to hear yourself speak above them if the table is too close to their residence, but no matter. The *Sully* is fun for anyone – except perhaps a sufferer from ornithophobia!

5

Paris to Beaune

It's always a good feeling when Paris is behind you and the bonnet is pointing South and in the direction of the wine country. There is a distinct sensation of getting somewhere, even though it is still getting on for 1,000km to Nice.

As you would expect from any main road close to a capital city, the **A6** going South is busy. The fact that it is the route to Orly Airport increases the traffic. Much of the road surface here is *rainurage* – a kind of concrete scored with lines which make grooves along the surface. Motor-bikes should beware on it, particularly in the wet, and my little Mini hated it. It seemed to disturb the balance of the wheels in some way, or maybe it was just that we bounced more. I had to slow down. The French apparently make some roads this way because they are supposed to last longer. My guess is that it also makes people drive more carefully. But once you get used to the different sound that driving on *rainurage* causes, in a full-sized car it is nothing to worry about.

When Fontainebleau is past, the *péage* looms and the **A6** is no longer free. A surprising amount of traffic instantly disappears, leaving those prepared to pay to bowl on through the wooded countryside that surrounds Fontainebleau.

Even if you resent paying, it is as well to stay on the autoroute between Nemour and Avallon, as the old roads veer off in the wrong direction. If you then come off at **Avallon** and take the **RN6** through **Saulieu**, **Arnay-le-Duc** and **Chalon-sur-Saône** it won't cost you a

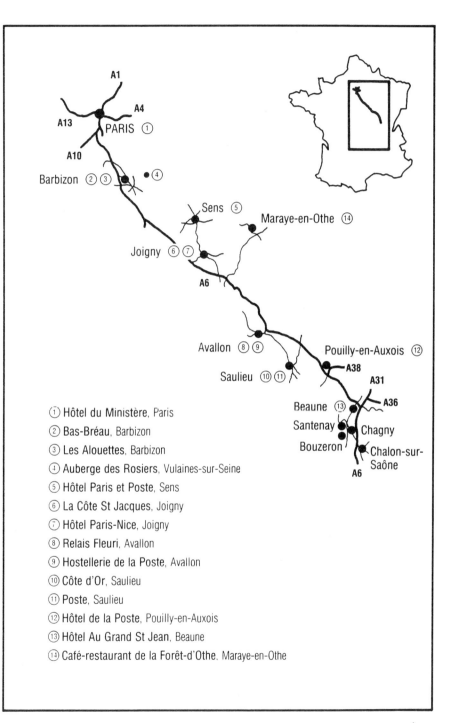

① Hôtel du Ministère, Paris
② Bas-Bréau, Barbizon
③ Les Alouettes, Barbizon
④ Auberge des Rosiers, Vulaines-sur-Seine
⑤ Hôtel Paris et Poste, Sens
⑥ La Côte St Jacques, Joigny
⑦ Hôtel Paris-Nice, Joigny
⑧ Relais Fleuri, Avallon
⑨ Hostellerie de la Poste, Avallon
⑩ Côte d'Or, Saulieu
⑪ Poste, Saulieu
⑫ Hôtel de la Poste, Pouilly-en-Auxois
⑬ Hôtel Au Grand St Jean, Beaune
⑭ Café-restaurant de la Forêt-d'Othe. Maraye-en-Othe

penny. This road is a few kilometres longer than the autoroute but is very beautiful, with wonderful sweeping views of Burgundy villages and châteaux. It is, of course, slower than the Autoroute du Soleil, as it bends about quite a bit and sometimes overtaking a slow vehicle can be difficult.

From **Chalon-sur-Saône** you could continue on the **RN6**, if you wish, right down to Lyon. But even though the road is not at all bad, I wouldn't if I were you. You will have to navigate through a number of towns, some large, such as Mâcon and Villefranche. The road isn't particularly attractive, either, though you drive through many villages with names familiar from wine bottles. It is hardly urban sprawl but there are a lot of houses, hotels, wine châteaux and, occasionally, light industry lining the highway. In high summer the whole area looks as if it needs dusting. The road is often two lanes, though with no central reservation, but there are stretches where it is three lanes and therefore a touch dangerous. It helps that most of these three-lane roads have a very positively defined dual carriageway going one way with a single carriage-way running in the opposite direction. After a mile or so, they swap. When using these three-lane highways, don't forget about not crossing the unbroken white line.

If, for financial reasons, you should decide to take the old road South, be sure to get back on the autoroute at Villefranche and take advantage of the free ride round Lyon. But really there isn't much point in not staying on the autoroute from Avallon through at least to Vienne, the other side of Lyon – even if you do have to pay. Unless, of course, you have plenty of time and fancy stopping at some of the many wine establishments where you can purchase direct from the grower. That's a different matter.

But let's retreat back to the South of Paris, where we sometimes stay on our return journey, so that we are fresh to face the Périphérique in the morning. Some people get this far in one day when travelling back, though it is a 928km drive from Nice. To achieve this means sticking to the autoroute and driving for at least seven hours. And that's without accounting for delays in Lyon. It really isn't to be recommended without two drivers.

If, however, you fancy stopping South of Paris,

Barbizon

Barbizon, 57km South of the capital and 9km from
Fontainebleau, is a good choice, but also a popular one. If
you want to stay at Barbizon in season, either stop driving
very early or book a room.

It's a little town, associated with painters and now very
classy, with many fine houses but little in the way of shops
or a high street. Being in Barbizon is somewhat like being
on a private estate outside Ascot. It has one superb and
very pretty hotel called the *Bas-Bréau*, which you
approach through an enchanting garden. We have been
inside and found it most elegant but never stayed there,
the reason being that if we stop at Barbizon it is always on
the way back, when funds are short. The conversation is
fairly predictable.

'Shall we stay at the *Bas-Bréau* this time?'

'It would be nice.'

'What's it going to cost?'

'Couple of hundred quid for the night.'

'How much have we spent already?'

'Shudder to think.'

'Shall we *not* stay at the *Bas-Bréau* this time?'

A room at the *Bas-Bréau* is £100 at least for the night
and a meal (one star) is £80 for two – and that's the
cheapest menu – so we have always given it a miss, particularly as there wouldn't be time to use either the pool
or the tennis courts or enjoy the huge, flowery garden at
the back. Our friend Vivienne Glenavy, the wife of the
late Patrick Campbell, who is a neighbour in France, loves
the *Bas-Bréau*. She and Paddy always stayed there on their
journeys back to England, so we mention it on her
recommendation.

Instead we stay round the corner at Monsieur Cresson's
Les Alouettes, a hotel that looks more like a higgledy-
piggledy house with a garden in front. We rather like it.
It's certainly not grand or exceptional in any way, but they
feed you well. I must admit that the bedrooms are totally
forgettable – but they must be OK, since one does not
forget acute discomfort. It also has the virtue of being
quiet and staying there costs from £18 to £35, all rooms
having a bath or shower (but only five have wcs.) When
we leave there we congratulate ourselves on having saved a
fortune!

This area outside Paris is extremely pretty. It is heavily

wooded. There are two rivers: the little Loing and the Seine, broad and peaceful, bending gently through small towns and smart villages, no doubt inhabited by rich Parisians. There are many riverside hotels as *tout Paris* comes here at weekends. We stumbled across the *Auberge des Rosiers* at **Vulaines-sur-Seine** when we were looking for somewhere else and it looked so pleasant we decided to stay. This *auberge* is a charming, small hotel right by the town bridge, with a perfect view over the river and a peaceful river walk in front. It is such a pleasant spot that it comes as no surprise to learn that both Toulouse-Lautrec and Ravel lived there for a while, two or three houses away from the hotel. The town itself is small and really not worth the walk along a busy road. But if you are content to wander by the river, watching the barges drift by in total silence, there is no nicer place to be.

The hotel appears quite contemporary, with a lot of light, polished wood and open staircases. Our sloping, high-ceilinged room, the last Madame Bourlier had left to offer, was spacious, with a view out over a garden and again with polished wood floors and rugs. It was simply but pleasantly furnished with a good, modern bathroom and lavatory.

When we went down to dinner, we were delighted to find that the restaurant was busy, and mostly with local people. It can be depressing eating in a deserted restaurant, but there was no possibility of that here. They were still welcoming diners when we left at about 9pm. The restaurant is smart and run by a head waiter of extraordinary presence. Smart in a white jacket, hair sleeked back and with a little moustache, he was serious and correct of demeanour. He walked with studied pace and his technique in opening a bottle of wine brought the urge to applaud. He was also extremely efficient. We both decided that at one time in his career he must have worked at the Ritz. Here was a man who was serious about his work, and it proved to be a serious restaurant.

The food was excellent. I happen to be very fond of *cervelle d'agneau*, another dish that, like *truite au bleu*, turns Philip pale. Since they were on the menu I ordered them. They were delicious: carefully prepared and cleaned in a way that is rare unless I do them myself at home. I had the lamb's brains and Philip had cutlets from the animal as our main courses. We were both content. The wine was reasonably priced – a rather good burgundy at £10 and the house cocktail, a Kir Royale, made with real champagne, was £3. Replete, we strolled along the river bank in the moonlight and with the light sparkling on the dark water Philip asked his famous question: 'I wonder if we could afford a little place here . . .'

There is no greater praise.

The only problem with the *Auberge des Rosiers* is that it is hell to get to. When we first found it we were going North and had left the autoroute at Fontainebleau. We had to drive through the town to pick up the **D210**. This proved surprisingly difficult and not to be undertaken unless you have a good map-reader in the car with you. The next time we found an easier way by coming off the autoroute much earlier – at the Sens exit – and we also discovered that Vulaines is much easier to get to when going South.

You'll find both routes described on page 179.

There is a bonus to all this. It is a very pretty drive through open countryside on those quiet roads, which come as such a relief after the speed and heavy traffic of the motorway. But with this particular hotel, having taken all that trouble to get there, it is wise to reserve in advance.

If all that map-reading and watching out for signposts puts you off, you could just simply come off the autoroute at the Sens exit, drive 23km on the **RN60** to join the **RN6** and stop at the *Hôtel de Paris et de la Poste* in **Sens**. You can't miss it. It is right where the **RN6** becomes the Rue République as it runs through the town.

It's a really nice old staid-looking hotel, well set back from the road, with a garden in front and only paces from the town's fine Gothic Cathedral. Inside it is cosy, with rustic charm. The *Paris et Poste* is not cheap but it is value for money. There is a tempting little bar where my husband once fell foul of an exuberant and thirsty Dutchman. Or maybe it was the Dutchman who fell foul of him. One thing is sure, that evening neither of them fully appreciated the excellent food the hotel serves in a country-style restaurant.

The hotel has been run by the Godard family for three

Sens

generations. The present Godard, Philippe, and his wife, Odile, have kept up the standards and you know you are in the hands of professionals the minute you walk through the door. Though the *Paris et Poste* is rather pricey, with rooms at about £40 for a medium priced double with bath, it is well worth the money and the 23km drive from the motorway.

About the same distance off the autoroute, 21km to be
Joigny   exact, is the town of **Joigny**, 146km from Paris. Joigny is a busy place but not particularly remarkable, though the beautiful Yonne river flows through its centre. What it does have is *A La Côte St Jacques*, a grand hotel that is one of France's few Michelin three-star restaurants. Like all three-star restaurants, *A la Côte St Jacques* is expensive, but, most people would agree, good value for what you get in the way of superb food and surroundings and skilled service. You feel like a millionaire at these restaurants, and I must say it helps if you are. But one of the better things about travelling in France is that, astronomically priced or really inexpensive, most establishments are value for money in their own way.

Our one and only, rather modest stop at Joigny proved that. In fact, it was more modest than we meant it to be. We had decided to stay at *Modern'H Frères Godard*, a hotel with a mouthful of a name, but with one star for food. We had an idea that it might be doing its best to catch up with the *A la Côte St Jacques* and therefore would be trying very hard. When we arrived they were desolate: the restaurant was closed. Tonight the hotel was host to the policemen's ball!

Disconcerted, we went looking for somewhere else, and found an extraordinarily ugly-looking little hotel, the *Paris Nice*, set on the edge of a roundabout. We went in via a squashed little bar that also held reception and, yes, they had a room, but those with bathroom (now at £20 the night) had all gone. Ours was one of the most basic kind – wash-basin and bidet behind a curtain. The loo was down the barely lit hall. It was one of those hotels where the electricity is so sparse one dare not use electric hair-curlers or a dryer. I did once in such an hotel and the embarrassment of plunging the entire building into darkness has stopped me trying it ever again. Philip takes a torch when we are economising and staying at the sort of hotel that itself economises on the electricity. Too often has he been left in darkness after a nocturnal visit to the loo when the time-switch has run out halfway down the hall.

We had a couple of drinks in a comic little bar which seemed popular with the locals and went into dinner. As usual the restaurant was cheerful and well lit, but the food was a bit special. The first course was an enormous helping of hors d'oeuvres. One served oneself and there were more than 30 delicious things to choose from. You could eat as much as you liked. They were equally generous with the main course and the cheese, and to Philip's delight there was chocolate mousse on the menu.

In the morning, our bill was £37, though I must emphasise that this was some years ago.

We drove on to Paris and booked in at the *Hôtel du Ministère*, a favourite, modestly priced, most pleasant little hotel near the Madeleine, and went for a stroll. As we wandered down the Rue St Honoré, on a sudden whim we walked into the Place Vendôme and into the Ritz. It was a lovely sunny Sunday morning, and we sat in their *chic* bar, looking over the charming garden outside, while I had two glasses of champagne and Philip had two Ricards – a Provence labourer's drink – each served with equal expertise. We both then had a perfectly prepared club sandwich. We had been cossetted in this gentle, relaxing ambience for about an hour when we called for the bill. Ceremoniously it was presented. It was £37 – exactly the same as our bill at the *Paris Nice*. And both were worth every penny.

Avallon

A more convenient stop than Joigny is **Avallon**. It is nearer the autoroute and, at 500km from Calais, is not exactly half-way but getting there. Somehow, quite frequently on our return journey we seem to find ourselves staying here, even though we hadn't intended it. In the days when I was driving alone and pushing myself because I was short of time before getting back to the office, I would find that it was at Avallon that I would begin to get tired and decide I had better stop. At just over 650km, having got on to the autoroute at Cannes, it was quite enough. With one driver, when coming North, it is less exhausting and safer to settle somewhere nearer Beaune.

Avallon has one advantage: the *Relais Fleuri*. This hotel is just a few kilometres from the autoroute, while being far

enough not to hear the noise of traffic rushing through the
night. Situated in the country outside the pleasant town, it
is a perfect stopping place: peaceful, inexpensive, comfortable and with reasonable though not spectacular food.

As you come off the autoroute and take the Avallon
road, you will find the *Relais Fleuri* set back from the road
on the right, on the corner of the **D94**. It's a pretty hotel,
comfortable without being pretentious, and looks like a
country house, set about with flowers. The lobby is spacious, with a bar where the *canapés* are out of this world,
and there is a swimming pool right outside. The lobby
leads into a surprisingly large, plainly furnished dining
room that always seems filled with people and full of bustle. It has the air, though not the ornate style, of a large
brasserie. One of life's embarrassing moments took place
here while we were having a pre-dinner drink. We overheard the arrival of a rather haughty English woman who
kept raising her voice in an effort to be understood. In the
end she demanded at the top of her lungs: 'Bring me
someone who speaks English.'

Oh dear.

The bedrooms at the *Relais*, motel-fashion, are separately built at the back of the hotel and you park your car
in front of your own front door. The rooms are exception-
ally comfortable, spacious and well-furnished, all with
TVs. They have sliding windows which give access to a bit
of a lawn. In these rooms the décor does not set your teeth
on edge. The colourings are soft – we always seem to get a
blue room – and the *en-suite* bathrooms are modern.

The food is hearty – no question of *nouvelle cuisine*.
They do a great *museau* (we'd call it chopped-up brawn in
Britain), which is one of Philip's favourites, and there
have been times when we have snuck off into Avallon for
a snack rather than face so much food after driving so far.
Driving takes away Philip's appetite. But if you are one
who finishes the journey ravenous, for you the *Relais
Fleuri* runs a great restaurant.

It's no hardship to take a run into Avallon. It is a cosy
town and an interesting one. It was once fortified, and the
ancient ramparts are worth a look. There is a calm about
the fine Church of St Lazare and its attendant ivy-clad
buildings which soothes after a long day on the road.
Often, too, there are colourful hot air balloons about.

There is a much more upmarket hotel in the town: the *Hostellerie de la Poste*. The rooms are luxurious, but many of them are over the old **N6** and noisy. In summer they are hot if you don't open the window, and if you open the window, beware of mosquitoes from the river and the traffic roar, which can go on all through the night. The food is excellent, but so elegantly *nouvelle cuisine* that one feels one ought not to interfere with it.

Saulieu

Before the autoroute was built, the pleasant town of **Saulieu** in the Côte d'Or was *the* stopping place on the great trek North and South. Now the **A6** bypasses it. Yet people must still make the effort to visit there, as it seems to support as many hotels as ever along the sprawling length of the town. And if, of course, you are taking the **RN6** to Chalon-sur-Saône and avoiding the autoroute, Saulieu is right on the route.

The main attraction in the town has always been the *Côte d'Or*, a most elegant hotel, which has three stars for food. It is not surprising that it is so popular. The *Côte d'Or*'s prices are low, for a hotel of such class and elegance. A double room is not much more than £60 for the night, with, of course, bath. The food is rather a different matter, costing up to £70 a head without wine.

More affordable is the *Poste*, on the corner of the Rue Grillot. This hotel has comfortable and stylish rooms and a pretty, smallish restaurant decorated in turn-of-the-century fashion. The only snag is that it is not particularly quiet, situated as it is on the corner of two main roads. So should you rest your head there ask for a *calme* room.

We enjoyed an excellent meal in the restaurant here until they brought the pudding. I had ordered fruit salad and when it was served I found a bowl of chopped up apple confronting me. In my terms that is not a fruit salad – not when the meal is costing £12 a head without wine. I sent it back and the waiter was quite sniffy. However, don't let the fact I do not like chopped apple put you off. You will have a very comfortable, well furnished room at the *Poste*, and a good meal. Just avoid the fruit salad.

Pouilly-en-Auxois

The *Poste* is quite grand; if you are looking for somewhere more simple in this neck of the woods, come off the autoroute at the **Pouilly-en-Auxois** exit. Drive into this nice little town and in the main square is the *Hôtel de la Poste*.

We have often stopped for lunch here, yet never stayed the night, but I am certain that Madame Bonnardot, the proprietor, will offer clean and comfortable rooms. Her rustic restaurant, obviously a favourite with the townsfolk, is impeccable and pleasantly decorated, in that sort of unobtrusive way that suggests the food is all-important – as indeed it is in Burgundy. Madame Bonnardot has Burgundian specialities on her menu: *escargots*, which Philip promptly ordered, and *jambon persillé*, one of my favourites. We don't see *jambon persillé* much in Britain. It is made with chopped chunks of good, unsmoked ham and sprigs of parsley set in a wine jelly. It is shaped like a loaf, cut in slices and served with baby pickled cucumbers. Delicious.

On our last visit we both had our favourite starter followed by *suprême de volaille*. With a bottle of white wine, ice-cream and coffee, the bill was under £25.

Beaune   Next stop **Beaune**, another city set close to the autoroute. Beaune, the capital of Burgundy, is beautiful, adorned with wondrous turreted buildings in checkerboard brick. Once there, the temptation is to spend hours wandering the narrow streets of the old city centre and admiring the fine architecture. Beaune needs time. As with Paris, it is best to make a special journey here and spend a few days exploring. To drive in at eventide and dash off at dawn is merely tantalising.

It is for this reason that in the normal way we never stay at Beaune but in the countryside nearby. We have only stayed in the town once, and it wasn't on one of our better trips. We had had a terrible row, though for the life of me I can't think what it was over. We had shared a delicious, but silent, £14-a-head lunch at *La Garbure* in **Châteauneuf-du-Pape** near Avignon (beautiful little town, very *chic* small hotel/restaurant, each room with bath, wc and TV for under £30. Must go back one day when we are both in a better temper) and driven on to Beaune, resentment steaming up the atmosphere.

It was late when we arrived and the first three hotels we tried were full. We finished up at the huge *Hôtel au Grand St Jean*, which was what you might call serviceable. It is a very large hotel with small, drearily furnished rooms, each one with its own bath and lavatory. Everything was perfectly clean, the bathroom adequate and there was a lock-up garage (£1.50). There were absolutely no frills, and it was extremely efficiently run by two brothers. The room for the two of us was just over £20, plus another £5 for our generous breakfasts, served in a barn of a room, but with great big bowls of butter on the table and still-hot bread. This is the sort of hotel that offers a family room with two double beds and bath, etc at £27.

The hotel does not have a restaurant, but Beaune is full of eating places, three of them with one star, so in fact, in retrospect the *Grand-St-Jean*, though definitely basic, is a sensible place to stay, particularly if you are on a budget.

Still not speaking, we went out to eat. There didn't seem much point in doing anything but falling into the nearest restaurant, which happened to be the *Pique Boeuf Grill*, where most of the cooking was done on a wood fire. Best I think to draw a veil over the food, but the bottle of Aligoté we ordered was excellent. It actually got us speaking again to the point where Philip suggested that if the Bouzeron establishment of Monsieur de Villaine, the producer of this wine, was near by, why didn't we go and buy some in the morning?

Bouzeron

Bouzeron was a little back on our tracks, just outside Chagny. We drove that magic Burgundy road (the **N74**) from Beaune back South, past Meursault and Puligny-Montrachet and Chassagne-Montrachet. The countryside, with the soft hills of the Côte and the symmetrical lines of vines that create some of the best wine in the world, is surprisingly beautiful. Coming from the North, it is worth driving the **N74** to just before Chagny, turning right on to the **N6** for about 8km and then picking up the **D973**, again on the right, which sweeps back North to Beaune. This road rings some of the finest vineyards in Burgundy and is a joy to drive. If you have time, do make the detour, or plan to stay somewhere locally. It is a good stopping point, since this part of Burgundy is more or less half-way from Paris.

It is easy to miss the **D219**, the tiny turning to Bouzeron. It is on the right, barely a kilometre to the South of Chagny. We missed it at the first attempt, then found the turning and drove through truly remote countryside. There was little to see, except some vineyards and a high verdant slope to the right. No sign of life until Bouzeron, a typical, crumbling Burgundy village, crept into view. There was a large and imposing château on the corner in the centre, but before going in we decided to have a coffee in the village café. That, too, was pretty basic, but Pat, the young woman in her frilly pinny, who ran the place, was helpful.

'Will they sell us some wine over there?' we asked.

She agreed they would, and then, dropping her voice, said: 'But it is better to go to Monsieur de Villaine. His prices are more reasonable.'

Since it was Monsieur de Villaine that we had been looking for all along, we were delighted, and Madame Pat instructed us to go to the house opposite and just ring the bell.

It was a lovely old house, built around a courtyard, and a young woman accompanied by a cheerful black labrador bitch came to let us in. She took us down into the cellars where we purchased a case of the wine we had drunk the night before, and with both of us in a rather better temper than previously, we set off for Paris.

When we went back later in the year, that wine had well and truly gone from our London store, so we thought that, as we were passing, we might as well purchase some more. It was nearing midday on a Sunday when we neared Chagny and Philip said: 'I suppose they'll be open on Sunday?'

'We can but try,' I said.

The labrador seemed to be waiting at the gate for us when we arrived, tail wagging like mad. And an elegant, tall man wearing a mac was in the courtyard, obviously just off somewhere.

'Could we buy some wine?' I asked, adding the obligatory *s'il vous plaît*.

He looked quickly at his watch.

'With pleasure,' he said, 'but I regret I have no time to offer you a tasting.'

I explained that we knew the wine very well and that a tasting was not necessary. After that we were in business.

We were dealing with Monsieur de Villaine himself, a man enthusiastic about his product. Aligoté, of course, is the name of the grape that produces the wine, and it has been grown in that little valley since the 12th century. Of all the Aligoté wine produced in Bourgogne only the Aligoté of Bouzeron had the coveted *appellation commu-*

nale, meaning that the growers are permitted to put Bourgogne Aligoté Bouzeron on their labels.

'The 1990 wine will be very good. It is fermenting now,' Monsieur de Villaine told us, 'but we have very little of it. Unfortunately, we had hail in May. And hail, of course, does terrible damage to young grapes.'

He packed us up 18 bottles, we paid him £63, and left, with him urging us to give him notice when we were coming back so that he could give us a proper tasting and show us around.

We went to visit Pat opposite again, and she poured us both a glass of excellent Aligoté, for which we were charged the vast sum of £1.60 for the two.

Burgundy is perhaps the best area to stop and buy wine on the journey, though it must be said it is not that much cheaper than in Britain. Really fine wine seems to cost much the same, but we do find that medium-priced wine works out less expensively bought at source. One saves perhaps £2 on a bottle if one shops carefully. Of course, there is a great deal more reasonably drinkable French plonk at about £1 a bottle than is to be found in Britain.

Santenay

It's also fun to do. We stop at the pretty little wine town of **Santenay**, where we visit Monsieur Mestre and his son at their establishment in the square. Their premises are a joy before you have even had a sip of wine: big and airy with wood floors and barrels and bottles all over the place. We are solemnly taken to the cellars in a lift, where, in near darkness, with a huge barrel for a table, we sample their wines. We usually buy La Doix wine, a rich red at about £5.50 a bottle, take it to Les Eygages and leave it under the stairs for a couple of years (alas we have no cellar) and, my goodness, it's wonderful when poured – and would have cost a great deal more in Britain. If one buys wine from an ordinary shop or a vineyard in France it is already taxed, so the British customs will allow you to bring home 8 litres of still wine (10 bottles each person) duty free. If you'd rather bring home champagne or a sparkling wine, you are only allowed 3 litres. If you want to mix the two, you may bring in 3 litres of sparkling and 5 litres of still.

Of course, you can buy more and pay duty, which is always £1.20 a litre for still wine and £1.99 a litre for sparkling, regardless of the price of the wine itself. If you buy from a duty free shop, this all changes, but quite honestly in our experience it is much better to buy wine duty paid. Spirits are a different matter. If you do buy your spirits duty paid, try to find a Leclerc supermarket, where the spirit prices are rock bottom – so much so that they ration the customers, and if you want to buy a lot, you have to keep going back and queuing again. If you are very far South, near Italy, it's worth making a trip to **Ventimiglia**, just over the border, where all wines and spirits are cheaper than in the cheapest duty free shop.

It is a great pleasure to visit a vineyard or a *cave*, where the owners are usually happy to give a tasting of their product. People who work with wine are invariably pleasant, and it makes us squirm when we see our own countrymen taking up a *vigneron*'s time and sloshing back his wine, only to finish up buying one or two bottles. The French never give the impression of minding, so maybe they don't. But it doesn't half embarrass us.

The wine country has a very special beauty and a curious kind of orderliness. The villages and small towns are neat, with their medieval conical turrets and yellow stone or red-brick and timber buildings. There is a profusion of rivers and the carefully tended vines create geometric patterns on the hillsides. But one sees little of this from the autoroute. In fact, I cannot recall one vineyard that is visible from the A6. To appreciate the awesome profusion of Bourgogne, it is necessary to drive the byways, even taking the C roads which run through the vineyards, where the grapes are often protected by stone walls which add to the drama of the view. The ancient wine villages, such as **Meursault, Volnay, Mercurey** and **Aloxe-Corton** are so silent that they seem to be sleeping off their own product.

But Burgundy has more than wine. What you will see as you drive through are fields of powerfully muscled, large, cream-coloured bulls. These are the famous Charolais cattle. Once they were only seen in the Burgundy district of Charolles; now they are bred throughout France.

Much of Grande Bourgogne, which includes the Yonne, is agricultural and a delight to the eye. One May we had driven from Cannes to the prosperous wine village of **Rully**, just outside Chagny in Bourgogne. Without leaving the autoroute the journey took six hours, one of which was spent in a traffic jam in Lyon.

The following morning, a Saturday, we set off on the **A6** again, but after a few kilometres, decided that we felt like driving through the countryside. The autoroute had been crowded the day before with traffic from 'the bridge' of the May bank holiday and we wanted some peace and quiet.

It was a glorious day and as, disappointingly, it had done nothing but rain in the South, we wanted to enjoy the sunshine. It must be said that May is often wet in the South. The joke in Cannes is that it invariably pours down all through the May film festival week and that you can't see the film stars for umbrellas. But this morning, so much further North, the sky was Alice blue, with a few puff-ball clouds, and Philip suggested that, just for fun, we work out a route that touched no RN roads and no large towns and that took us round to the East of Paris, avoiding the Périphérique.

It took some doing, but the result was spectacular. Of course the weather helped, and it didn't hurt that huge fields of rape and mustard were blooming like a vast, bright yellow eiderdown spread all over the countryside, but I think it fair to say that this was one of the most beautiful drives we have ever made.

On the route we chose, there was hardly any traffic at all. We drove alongside slow-moving canals and fast-running little rivers such as the Armançon. We skirted great vistas of open land, forests, dramatic escarpments of white rock and ranges of soft hills as well as many, many charming little villages. And as we neared Champagne there was the occasional hillside of orderly vines. This is a prosperous area of France and there is absolutely nothing ugly to be seen.

The journey took a long time. We left at 9am and arrived in Arras, where we stayed the night, at 6pm. But we could have pushed on and caught a boat if it had been necessary. With so little traffic, the drive was not tiring. On the way, we stopped for a drink at a sleepy riverside village called **Cry**, and again for lunch at 1pm. There was also a petrol stop for penny-spending and a brief walkabout. This is not a journey to undertake if you are in a hurry. But if you have the time, if the sun is shining, the rape is blazing, and you feel like by-passing Paris, you'll find how we did it, taking a national route only at the very end of the journey, on page 179.

Maraye-
en-Othe

If you do pass this way, please stop off at the *Café-Restaurant de la Fôret d'Othe* at **Maraye-en-Othe**. We only stopped there because on these quiet roads on a bank holiday Saturday, we couldn't find anywhere else. But lunch there proved to be a French experience we wouldn't have missed for the world. The *Café-Restaurant de la Fôret* is a long, low building on the right as you enter the village from the South. You can't miss it: there is nothing else to distract from it. *Crêpes* are advertised on the wall outside, and I thought we would have to settle for this overrated Normandy dish for lunch. Rubbery *crêpes*, usually full of something indistinguishable and indigestible, are not family favourites. Not a bit of it. Inside a room with bare wooden tables and an amazing amount of clutter on the walls, the proprietors, Monsieur and Madame Claud Kiry, were standing shoulder-to-shoulder, leaning on the brightly lit bar at the back of the room, two glasses of what seemed to be Ricard set before them. Small people of what the French call politely 'certain age', they looked like a pair of weather-dolls. Apart from them, the place was deserted.

Did they serve lunch? I asked after the *politesses* had been made.

'But, of course,' said Madame, raising well-plucked eyebrows at such a stupid question.

Any port in a storm. I shot out to tell Philip the good news and by the time we had parked, Madame had already prepared a table in another, even more cluttered room, to which she led us with great solicitude.

As we looked nervously at the muddle of it all, she announced 'I am going to take very great care of you.'

And she did.

We must, she said, first of all refresh ourselves with her cider. She had in her hand a green bottle with no label. In the other were two old-fashioned champagne glasses which she filled with some ceremony and placed before us. It was thirsty work, driving, she said. And yes, she appreciated that we had to continue driving, but we must not be unquiet. There was not a drop of alcohol in her cider. She added that to drink with our meal, she would bring a bottle of good, red Côtes du Ventoux, and added: 'Now the food.'

As she bustled off, neat as a pin in her pink woolly jumper and a white skirt, short enough to show off a good pair of legs, her husband, out in the bar, was changing the music to a song by the Beatles.

'In our honour?' Philip asked, as we sipped cautiously at the cider. It was excellent, though when she returned and beamed to find we had drunk it, insisting that we had another glass, we rather doubted her assurances that it was *sans alcool*.

There was no question of a menu. We were given an hors d'œuvre consisting of *crudités* and a mixture of fish, including little squid and some shrimps. It was good. Madame had obviously made the mayonnaise herself. The main course was truly magnificent. Madame arrived bearing two steaming, spice-scented dishes. One was piled with *petit pois*, cooked in the traditional way with tiny onions, a touch of lettuce and a lot of the smoked pork fat so essential to French peasant cooking. In the other dish were two large duck legs in a rich but pale-coloured sauce. Duck can be tough. But this just fell from the bone in succulent strips. Chewing was not required. It tasted wonderful. Again, the dish had been larded and flavoured with the smoked pork fat, and there was another vegetable within the sauce which tasted like asparagus. But no: it was salsify.

This was no dish of refinement, but robust, full of flavour and something to give a health-food faddist a fit. It was memorable and rare in these days of *nouvelle cuisine*. We made pigs of ourselves.

We congratulated Madame Kiry as she stood shaking her head because we had not made a big enough dent in the bowl of *petit pois*. To take her mind off this disappointment, I asked how she had cooked the duck.

'It was marinated in champagne, with the salsify, for many hours,' she said, pleased to be asked. 'Then cooked, so slowly in the champagne, for many hours also. It was good?'

'Excellent.'

'Ah, *bon!*'

She brought in a platter of cheese which she left in front of us. Before she left she gave the Bleu de Bresse and the Pont l'Evêque a contemptuous prod.

'You do not want these. Try this one,' she said, pointing to a large, round cheese, 'it is local. And this. A *fromage blanc* that I made myself. It is, as you see, more solid than those one buys.'

The local cheese was called Chaource Dugerot, and it was creamy without being runny and had its own positive, rather fruity flavour. It was very good. Her home-made *fromage blanc* was equally good, solid enough to spread on bread. Again we made pigs of ourselves, and, when she came to remove the cheese-dish, apologetically cried off any dessert.

It was a waste of breath. Madame was taking great care of us and we were not leaving without eating the pudding she had prepared. She returned bearing pots of home-made apple sauce served with a slice of feather-light sponge cake: also home-made. We ate all that, too.

'You are a fine chef, Madame,' Philip told her when she came with the coffee.

She laughed.

'I have been cooking for 40 years. I am content with my life and my work. What more do I need, now I am no longer young?' But the flirty little look she gave Philip gave the game away: she didn't really believe she was too old for anything.

'You pass this way often?' she asked us.

We had to say no.

'But your friends?'

'Ah, maybe,' I said.

'It is possible to stay here. We have rooms. Rooms with everything you could desire.'

'WC?' I asked with a smile, trying to make a joke of it so that she would not be offended. I had reason to ask. Philip had made the customary reconnaissance and discovered only the dreaded hole in the ground at the back.

'Of course. Everything that anyone could desire. And,' she paused for dramatic effect, 'your friends can stay here, full *pension*, breakfast, lunch, dinner and the room for 150 francs a day.'

Full board for £15 a day? Our faces must have shown that we found this hard to believe, for she raced into the bar, came back with a postcard of the village, and wrote down the figure.

'Of course,' she said, as she stamped the address and telephone number of the restaurant on the card with a rubber stamp. 'We are mad. Everyone says so. All meals and a bed for so little.'

Well, I don't know about mad, but Madame Kiry was certainly not greedy. The coffee was on the house, and our meal, with the cider and a bottle of 1986 Côtes du Ventoux came to less than £20.

For the young, the hard-up and the adventurous, wanting to explore somewhere off the tourist tracks, Madame Kiry's establishment might prove to be a lot of fun to stay at, since she herself was such fun.

And we would certainly make a diversion to enjoy again her wonderful, old-fashioned French cooking. You don't come across it much these days.

6

Beaune to Lyon:
The Wine Road

Almost anywhere in Burgundy is a good place to stop
for a night on your journey. Beaune is exactly half-way to
Nice from Calais and, if you only push on a little further,
the back of the journey is broken. And, of course, it is a
lovely part of the world in which to relax for a while.

Chalon-sur-Saône

Chalon-sur-Saône is nicely convenient. It has two
motorway exits, one at the North of the town and one at
the South, so you can enter one way and come out the
other, thus cutting out the need to retrace your steps when
leaving. Only 26km from Beaune, Chalon is a good-sized
town, without being large enough to get you desperately
lost. The broad river Saône runs through the centre, and
if you want to stretch your legs there are pleasant walks
both along the river and in the fascinating old town off the
Quai des Messageries.

It is a lively place. There always seems to be something
going on. Chalon has a pleasure harbour where boats can
be hired for a chug up the river; there is a memorable rose
garden; one can go hot-air ballooning there. The
Chalonnais are said to give the best nine-day Carnival in
all of France in February or March, with a masked parade
on both the Sundays. No time for these? How about a
visit to the House of Wine, where you can taste after a
small payment and buy the 44 wines that are grown on the
Côte Chalonnaise? Set in a lovely old wooden building
with an ornamental balcony running all round, it is on the

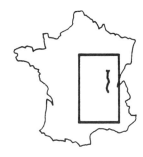

Beaune

A6 A31
A36

④ Chagny ③
Chalon-sur-Saône ① ②
Givry ⑤

A6 Tournus ⑥ ⑦ ⑧
Pont-de-Vaux ⑨

⑬ A40
Mâcon ⑩ ⑪ ⑫

Villefranche-sur-Saône
⑮ ⑯ ⑰

A6 LYON

⑭

① Hôtel St Jean, Chalon-sur-Saône
② Le St-Georges, Chalon-sur-Saône
③ Lameloise, Chagny
④ Hôtel-restaurant du Commerce, Rully
⑤ Hôtel-restaurant de la Halle, Givry
⑥ Hôtel de Greuze and Restaurant Greuze, Tournus
⑦ Terminus, Tournus
⑧ Le Sauvage, Tournus
⑨ Hôtel Joubert, Pont-de-Vaux
⑩ Bellevue, Mâcon
⑪ Mercure, Mâcon
⑫ Novotel, Mâcon
⑬ Relais du Mâconnais, La Croix Blanche
⑭ Mercure, Chasse-sur-Rhône
⑮ Hôtel Plaisance, Villefranche-sur-Saône
⑯ La Fontaine Bleue, Villefranche-sur-Saône
⑰ Brasserie du Rhône, Villefranche-sur-Saône

Promenade Sainte-Marie, open daily 8am to 12.30pm and 1.30pm to 8pm.

We once arrived in Chalon on Bastille Day, the 14th of July, to find the whole town on the streets having a good time. A fun-fair had been set up on the Quai, the children were in fancy dress, and there was a moped and a bicycle race going on. Chalon was *en fête* in brilliant sunshine. It was fun and it was noisy, so when we checked into the little *St Jean* hotel (inexpensive, no restaurant, smart, clean and functionally modern) we sensibly asked for a room at the back.

It was a nice big room with a good bathroom. Tired, we went to bed early, only to find that we had not chosen well. At midnight the firework display began incorporating all those spectacular bangs, crashes and brilliant tableaux of fire that the French expect from their *feu d'artifice*. Sudden silence descended at 1am. Unfortunately, this all took place at the back of the hotel and what felt like right in front of our window. It could have been a sight to remember, if we had not been too tired to get out of bed and watch.

If Philip and I have only had a snack lunch on our journey, we like to stay at the *St-Georges* hotel in Chalon, for a very good reason. The restaurant of the hotel has one Michelin star: a well deserved star that is a wasted experience if we have eaten too well at lunchtime. The hotel is very near the station, but don't let this put you off. We have never so much as heard a train whistle in the night and the location does make the hotel easy to find. One simply follows the signs for *Gare* or *SNCF* (Société Nationale des Chemins de Fer Français). The hotel has recently been completely refurbished, and not before time. It had become a little shabby, which made the rooms overpriced. With brand new décor in every room, a double with bath costs about £38; with shower, £33. It is a large old hotel, reminiscent in its faded grandeur of a British Rail hotel.

The restaurant is elegant, the service impeccable, and the food delicious. It is one of those restaurants where the lighting and the ambience make for a feeling of well-being. One should dress up a little for the *St-Georges*: this is high-class cuisine and though the lowest priced meal is not unreasonable at about £14 a head (without wine) it is

worth splashing out here. One of their specialities is
ravioli made with lobster and prawns. And, of course,
they have an excellent wine list.

In its own way, *Le St-Georges* is value for money. So is
a much smaller establishment a few miles down the road,
the *Hôtel-Restaurant du Commerce* in the wine village of
Rully. We arrived here by rather an odd route. We had
been four thousand miles away in St Bart's in the French
Caribbean, talking to a homesick restaurant-owner from
Chagny in Burgundy. He was thrilled to bits to meet
someone who knew his home territory. He knew
Monsieur de Villaine at Bouzeron well, and we discussed
the relative merits of the Côte Chalonnaise wines. And he
spoke nostalgically of his time working at the *Commerce* in
Rully. It was only a simple village hotel/restaurant, but
charming, he assured us.

Six months later we were nearing Chagny and, opti-
mists that we are, had the impulse to treat ourselves to a
stay at the three-star *Lameloise*. This is one of the most
beautiful hotels in France, owned by Jacques and Nicole
Lameloise, who say, and truthfully, that one does not
simply eat at their hotel: one tastes, one savours and one is
left moved by emotion. Apart from that, the big white
house, placed to face down Chagny's high street, is furnished with antiques and original fabrics and is quite
beautiful.

But of course, they were fully booked. Madame was
desolate, but even the restaurant was fully booked. Since
the other reasonable hotels in Chagny do not have restaurants, there seemed no point in remaining. We do like the
cheap and cheerful *Poste* just across the road from the
Lameloise, as it is tucked down a long alley and very tranquil, but the *Poste*, also, was *complet*. Which was not surprising, since it was the May bank holiday weekend.

'Let's try the one in Rully that chap in St Bart's told us
about,' Philip suggested.

Rully is about 4km off the **D981** out of Chagny and the
village and the *Hôtel du Commerce* are signposted to the
right, going South, just after the turning for Bouzeron.
We were there in no time and weaving through the prosperous village, where every other building seemed to
have something to do with wine.

We found the *Commerce* in the village square – a handsomely fronted, well kept building with parking in a large open space behind. We peered through the geraniums into the restaurant and decided it looked OK. A notice sent us to the side entrance, which led into a lobby with a huge open fire and comfortable squashy seats. As soon as we put our heads around the door a tall young man in a chef's apron and hat came from the kitchen. Carefully wiping his hands on a cloth, he checked the register. He had two rooms left. One *très simple* and one with a *douche* (shower). We said we would have the one with the shower.

He took us to see the room up two flights of a tightly curving old staircase. The room had little in common with the Ritz. Two beds, one large, one small, with wallpaper and bedcovers both best forgotten. It was furnished with a chest of drawers and wardrobe belonging to no discernible period. There was a loo and a tin shower squashed in a cubicle. In other words, it was exactly like thousands and thousands of inexpensive French hotel rooms. But this room had a casement window that opened out to a peaceful view of gardens, roof-tops and the sound of bird-song. We took it.

We had an hour before dinner was served and we couldn't find a bar in the village anywhere – 'Wine, wine everywhere, and not a drop to drink,' Philip said cheerfully, as we fell back into the car and drove to Bouzeron to see Pat in the bar there for a glass of her Aligoté. Should you ever stay in Rully, do make this short countryside drive. At the end of the village you will see a signpost to Bouzeron and, if you follow this narrow road, the views are spectacular, around a great wooded hill, through miles of wines, and presenting sweeping vistas of the cliff which protects the vines. Lovely. And a good glass of wine at the end of it in one of the most unpretentious bars you have ever seen – but truly French.

We were back at the *Commerce* spot on 7pm and panting for our meal, having skipped lunch with the *Lameloise* in mind. We were not the first in the dining room. Others were waiting in the big, light, pleasantly furnished room with tables set well apart. There was an air of expectancy and a very good aroma coming from the kitchen. We were about to find that, in common with many simple French hotels, food was what the *Commerce* was all about.

A rather shy, very young lass was serving everyone. She

lit the candle on the table and as she handed us the menu
suggested timidly we might like to try the house aperitif at
£2. This was made with sparkling wine and *marasquin*, a
sort of black cherry liqueur, and to order it seemed the
right thing to do, as Rully is well-known for its *crémant*
wines. In fact, the wine-makers of the village claim that
they rocked the cradle of *méthode champenoise* wines. For
160 years they have had the reputation for producing a
light, fresh *vin mousseux*, which is a champagne substitute.
If, that is, you can bring yourself to believe that champagne has a substitute. I personally felt that the
marasquin made our aperitif too sweet. Philip, who has a
sweeter tooth, quite liked it.

The wine list was surprisingly inexpensive. All the
aperitifs, apart from the special, were £1.60; all digestifs
£2.70. For £18 there was a real champagne on offer from
Bouzy – another aptly named village in Champagne where
they also make excellent red wine.

Not surprisingly, most of the wines were Côte
Chalonnaise and we chose a red Rully 1986 *premier cru*. It
cost a tenner, was light, without a lot of body, but very
pleasant. We resisted a Chassagne-Montrachet '87 at £19,
though we agreed it was not overpriced. Rully is better
known for light, fruity white wine, but we felt red would
be better with the *coq-au-vin* that Phil had ordered.

The cheapest menu was about £7 for salad or cream of
mussel soup, followed by a chicken dish or fillets of rose
trout. Both cheese and sorbet were included. We settled
for the £10 menu. Philip had his favourite *escargots* served
in layers of puff-pastry and I had the most wonderfully
creamy chicken pâté. There was a choice of escalope of
salmon cooked in the *crémant* wine, *coq-au-vin* or, my own
choice, duck with *mousseron* mushrooms – another of the
many varieties of fungus that the French eat so cheerfully.
It is a pity we British are so timid about mushrooms, since
most of those that the French eat do grow in our country.
The late Robert Graves had a theory that our national
alarm at being confronted by most forms of fungi is
caused by a hangover from the days when only Druid
priests were permitted to eat certain mushrooms because
of their hallucinatory powers.

I have never found that any of the various *champignons*
that the French serve had that effect, though my godchild

once found some on Hampstead Heath that did, but these
unknown varieties can be more flavourful than ordinary
mushrooms. They are much sought after in the French
countryside, where they are food for free. Indeed, some
pharmacies in rural districts sell a colourful poster with
drawings of every kind of fungi, describing them and,
most importantly, explaining which are edible and which
are poisonous.

Mousserons are tiny mushrooms that we do not see in
Britain, and their delicate flavour was excellent with the
duck. Philip polished off his *coq-au-vin* and we then
polished off cheese and dessert. It was a generous £10-
worth and we were glad that we had not chosen the £15
menu. This offered more choice and another course. We
were replete with what we had eaten and after lingering
over coffee, we took ourselves up what really was a
wooden hill and went to bed.

Truthfully, the beds could have been more comfortable, but the silence encouraged sleep. I was woken early
by birdsong, never an unpleasant way to greet the day,
and there was plenty of hot water in the Heath Robinson
shower.

For breakfast, Monsieur Lollini provided a glass of not
very pleasant orange squash along with good coffee and
the best croissant that we had eaten for a long time –
buttery, fluffy, feather-light. He proved to be both chef
and proprietor and had been at the *Commerce* for only
three months, so he did not know our friend from the
Caribbean. In fact, so new was he that he did not take
credit cards. He apologised as we dug around for £60 in
real money, assuring us that he would have the facility
next time we came. It wasn't an idle promise: he now
takes major credit cards. He also plans to improve the
bedrooms in time and we would certainly go again.

Not far away from the *Commerce* – 11km further South
and 13km off the autoroute, whether you leave from the
North or the South of Chalon-sur-Saône, is the wine town

Givry

of **Givry**.

In this charming, small town is another of our favourite
stopping places, the *Hôtel-Restaurant de la Halle*. Though
the hotel has 10 rooms, we have never stayed. We have
lunched there many times and have no doubt that the
rooms, priced from under £20, each with bath and wc,

would be smart and clean if the gleaming, loved restaurant is anything to go by. There, you can choose between £8, £14 or £18 menus.

Monsieur Renard, a man who is a stickler for detail, runs his restaurant with great style, keeping a sharp eye on both his staff and customers to make sure everything is right. There was an occasion when an imperious lady was becoming highly agitated because she wanted the bill while most of the clients were still being served. Monsieur Renard informed her with icy courtesy that those who had not eaten came before those who had. He is perhaps a touch autocratic, but who cares, when his devotion to his restaurant creates such a pleasing ambience and such jolly good food.

The hotel is easy to find, as it sits opposite an interesting, round, ancient market building which now houses the *Bureau de Tourisme*. The dining room itself is quite small – long and with room for one four-seater table each side with a passage-way down the centre. It has a most attractive counter at the head of the restaurant as you enter. Also on display are some of the *hors d'œuvres*, such as fat Breton artichokes in season, and wonderful golden-yellow apple tarts for dessert. If you plan lunch there, arrive early; we have never seen the *Halle* with an empty table.

Givry is still in Grand Bourgogne, and Monsieur Renard has my favourite *jambon persillé*, *escargots*, quiches and Burgundy dishes on his menu. On one occasion we were fortunate enough to arrive when a savoury rabbit stew was on the menu.

Monsieur Renard has a fine selection of Givry wine, which apparently was *the* favourite wine of the French King Henry IV. Henry had good reason. We have drunk some really pleasing full-bodied local red wines here that have a fascinating nose of *herbes de Provence*: wines which are not well known in Britain and which are very reasonably priced.

It is only comparatively recently in the history of wine that these Côte Chalonnaise wines – Givry, Rully, Aligoté, Mercurey and Montagny – have become popular. White Montagny has, indeed, become very expensive. For many years the Côte Chalonnaise was the Côte d'Or's neglected little sister, but the remarkable efforts of Jean-François Delorme, the son of a Rully grower, changed all that. He

expanded his own vineyards and researched the best
methods of making wine from the Pinot Noir and
Chardonnay grapes which grow on the secluded Côte
Chalonnaise hills. This created a resurgence of interest in
the wines, which hadn't been well regarded since Henry.
And it is Monsieur Delorme who popularised the *crémant*
wines which Monsieur Lollini uses in his house aperitif.

Since Givry and Rully are so close, which to choose?
Though Givry is larger and livelier than Rully – as much
as any small French town is lively – we would plump for
the *Commerce* at Rully as an overnight stop, the *Halle* for a
lunchtime stop. The *Halle* is busy, bustling and good
value – you can eat there for as little as £8. It is fun for
lunch when a bit of stimulation is required. But we'd
definitely go for the village peace and calm of the
Commerce for a night's stay – even if the beds could be
bettered.

From village to small town to serious town. Continuing
Tournus   South, 27km from Chalon, the twin towers of **Tournus**
are suddenly visible from the autoroute, immediately sig-
nalling where you are. Tournus is not *that* large, with
under seven thousand inhabitants, but it is remarkably
well served for hotels and restaurants. It is also only
minutes off the autoroute, so stop here early if you have
not reserved. Other people get the same idea.

This mellow old town has a lovely riverside frontage
and an ancient abbey and church. Off the main road it is a
pleasure to wander here. The busy old **N6** forms the
town's main street, and no doubt the autoroute came as a
blessing to the inhabitants. But long before the **A6** was
even thought of, Tournus was famous as the home of the
Hôtel de Greuze and the *Restaurant Greuze*.

With these establishments we are back in the upper
price bracket. Both are extremely expensive, and personally I have never seen the point of paying more than £100
a night plus £8 for a continental breakfast to stay at an
hotel that sits right on a main road. If you are looking for
unadulterated luxury, stay here. But if you can't get a
room at the back, forget it.

The restaurant is equally expensive. Expect to pay anything from £30 to £50 a head, without wine. But it is
beautiful, large, cool and yet light and airy, with stone
walls and that confident, calm atmosphere of a top-class

restaurant. I ate lunch here for the first time on that same occasion as I stayed the night in a *café des sports* in Compiègne. I had gone to bed with no supper and had no breakfast, having left the café at crack of dawn, and was starving by the time I reached Tournus at about 12.30pm.

As the twin towers appeared, I began to think about food. A few quick sums convinced me that I could afford the *Greuze*, having paid £4 for a hotel room and nothing for food the previous day. 'To hell with the expense,' I decided, and came off the **A6** to drive into Tournus, where the hotel, looking not unlike a Cotswold building, is on the right (going South) half-way down the main street.

Considering I was a lone woman, looking pretty scruffy, not having bathed and having driven since early morning, the hotel staff could not have been more charming. I was given a pleasant table and a drink and was fussed over. Having pored long over the menu, mentally wincing at the prices, I decided on *saumon éminence* as my main course. Stupidly, I did not ask exactly what it was.

When the dish arrived, elegantly presented on a large porcelain plate, I learned that *saumon éminence* is just another name for gravlax, something I thoroughly dislike. I had vaguely thought I was getting something like a salmon fishcake. As, however, this large helping of raw salmon was costing me near enough £20 I jolly well made myself eat it. It was a lesson always to ask for a description if you are not quite certain of the contents of a dish. It wasn't the *Greuze*'s fault I dislike gravlax. I had no reason to send it back.

Much more down-to-earth is the *Terminus* restaurant, right next to the station and also on the main street. To be truthful, we really prefer it to the *Greuze*. In the *Greuze* you could be in any expensive restaurant almost anywhere in the world. At the *Terminus* you are indisputably in France.

It has a big old bar-room for the locals with a turn-of-the-century mirrored bar, reminiscent of a drawing by Toulouse Lautrec, as you go in. The large, spick-and-span restaurant is always busy. Not surprising, since you can eat a hearty meal there for around £7 a head without wine, and they have a very reasonable house wine at just over £4. One can stay here in a double room for less than £20.

We have never chanced it. With the railway behind and the **N6** in front, a peaceful night's sleep seems unlikely. But for those who can sleep through anything it is worth a try on the grounds of economy, if nothing else.

Between the elegance of the *Greuze* and the simplicity of the *Terminus* comes *Le Sauvage*, which also has the virtue of being off the main road and away from the station. It is a most attractive old house, converted into an hotel and part of the Best Western group. You'll find it in the Place du Champs-de-Mars, which is off the main street on the left (going South). We have neither stayed nor eaten there, but we have friends who always make for this one-time *grande maison*. They like the fact that each room has a mini-bar and television, and they say the regional cuisine (still Burgundian) is excellent and the wine list remarkable. It is a second-hand recommendation, but I mention it since it slots in neatly between the establishments with which we are familiar.

Coming South off the **A6** at Tournus gives another possibility. Stay on the **N6** through the town and drive on for another 14km. Just after the straggling town of **Fleurville** there is a turning on the left, the **D933**, which goes to **Pont-de-Vaux**. This little town sits tranquilly on the river Reyssouze, a tiny tributary of the Saône.

Pont-de-Vaux

Pont-de-Vaux is charming. It has a big square where there are several pleasant cafés and a busy main street with quite a few shops, some devoted to the needs of those who fish or shoot. The average Frenchman is potty about fishing, and this activity is important to Pont-de-Vaux. It is the main reason why people visit the town.

We booked into the *Joubert* hotel in the Place Général Joubert, a fairly typical moderately priced hotel which at one time must have been a coaching inn. It still has a courtyard, where there is now private parking. Our welcome was good. We were greeted by a friendly young woman, who insisted on taking our overnight bag upstairs and asked if we would be in for dinner.

It was tempting to say 'no', since a Pont-de-Vaux restaurant, *Le Raisin*, has one Michelin star, but when staying at a small hotel it always seems discourteous to eat elsewhere. This type of hotel relies on its restaurant takings, rather than on earnings from accommodation. In fact, simple as the rooms are, we are always astonished that they cost so little. And it never seems unreasonable to us when the proprietors only let rooms to those who are taking dinner, since so much loving care invariably goes into the food.

The *Joubert* only has 16 rooms, and an ordinary double room with bath is around £25. Our room overlooked the square and was pleasant enough without having much that was memorable about it. But we knew from the scents rising from the kitchen that the food was going to be fine. We marvelled again at how rare it is in France to smell that sickly, oily smell of cheap cooking-fat that pervades every tourist spot in Britain: a smell that gets into the hair and the clothes and lingers for days. At the *Joubert* the atmosphere was of garlic and butter and onions with a touch of cinnamon. We sniffed appreciatively.

We washed and wandered out into a town flooded with sunshine. Running off the main street was an interesting little alley, which took us down to the Reyssouze. This is only a tiddler of a river, criss-crossed with small wooden bridges and trickling cheerfully along behind houses and gardens. The far bank is purposeful with allotments, though the allotment owners appeared to be more into growing flowers than vegetables for the table. Great bursts of sunflowers were the favourites.

Back on the main street, the road turned on to a proper bridge, where two fishing inns waited attendant on the river. We hung idly over this bridge, peering for trout in the shallow water. Others were also looking for trout. Below us were two unattended fishing rods.

'They'll have gone for a drink,' said Philip, pointing downwards. 'And look, one of them has caught a fish.'

So he had. A float was bobbing frantically and gradually disappearing under the bridge. There was no sign of the angler.

'He's going to lose it if he doesn't get out of the pub,' Philip remarked.

When time is unimportant, small things can become of consequence. We became riveted by this float bobbing in the cool, sparkling green of the river. It disappeared under the bridge and then reappeared and bobbed upstream, zig-zagging as the unfortunate but powerful fish tried to free itself. Still no-one came.

We watched for a good 10 minutes, enjoying the

warmth of the sun on our backs. When the float vanished
yet again under the bridge we wandered on, wondering if
we should pop into the fishing inn and inform the chap
that he was about to lose his catch. In the end, we decided
to leave it all to fate, and by the time we walked back to
the bridge the float was at peace, the fish was free and the
rods still unattended.

'He'll never know what he missed,' said Philip.

On that same bridge was a small memorial plaque to
men of the town who, when working for the French
Resistance, had been caught and shot by the Germans on
the bridge, while the gentle river flowed beneath. They
had been assassinated on the last day of the war. But they
were not forgotten: fresh flowers marked the place where
they had died. We walked back to the hotel, moved to
silence.

The big dining room overlooking the square was
already quite busy, and we noted that, as usual, more
attention had been paid to the décor of the restaurant than
to the bedrooms – and a lot more attention to the food.
The menus run from as little as under £10 to £25 a head.
We went for the middle menu. I ate their *foie-gras* and
Philip had mussels and, seeing as we were in a fishing
area, we both went for the freshwater *sandre*, a sort of
delicate pike.

We had only been seated for a moment when a group of
eight Frenchmen arrived and were seated at a table on our
left. Each punctiliously said 'Monsieur-'dame,' to us before sitting down. They were all casually but tidily dressed
and all very bronzed.

'Fishermen?' I whispered.

'Probably,' said Philip.

'No wives. Bet they've said they're on a business trip.'

'And gone fishing.'

'Or shooting,' I said as a second guess.

We all got on with our *hors d'œuvres*, the party of men
trying to speak quietly so as not to monopolise the acceptable level of noise. By the main course and several bottles
of wine later their voices were rising and great gales of
laughter reverberated around the restaurant. No-one else
seemed to mind. They were having such a good time, and
the atmosphere was good-natured. Smiles were spreading
across the faces of the other diners.

By the cheese the men were singing, and they continued to sing, surprisingly melodiously, right through to the coffee and liqueurs. Occasionally we were thrown an apologetic look, and occasionally they sang an English song. *Greensleeves* was one. The bronzed faces were becoming redder but never for one moment did we feel it would all end in tears. They were still singing when we went to bed.

They straggled into the breakfast room the following morning in varying degrees of disarray.

'How are your heads?' I asked as we left and received a concerted groan in reply.

They left the hotel at the same time as we did, all suddenly transformed, wearing those brilliantly coloured, skin-tight Latex cycling suits that Frenchmen sport – except that we realised, when we saw the car that was accompanying them and their bikes, that these men were Swiss cyclists and a long way from home.

'It's flatter here,' Philip pointed out as we waved them goodbye.

Pont-de-Vaux was lovely. We promised ourselves that we'd return.

Mâcon In this area it makes a lot more sense to stay somewhere like Pont-de-Vaux than to stop off at Mâcon. **Mâcon** is a big town with North and South exits. On the one occasion we did stay there we were both still at full-time work and time was short. To avoid getting lost we were careful to stick to the **N6**, which runs right through the town and alongside the river. We also chose an hotel on the river, both for the view and because we would be on the right road the following morning. It's easy to waste time getting lost in the middle of a town this size.

The *Bellevue*, where we stayed, is on the Quai Lamartine, 6km off the autoroute coming from either North or South. It is quite small, with only 25 rooms, an old hotel that has been carefully modernised but without taking away any of the character. It is one of the Best Western group. The rooms are traditionally decorated, and ours, right at the top of the hotel, was small but very pretty, with *toile-de-joie* wallpaper and nice pieces of antique furniture. The bathroom was also small, but adequate. Perhaps most importantly, the rooms are all double-glazed against the noise of the big city.

Philip liked the civilised bar, where we could sit and
have a drink before dinner. Comfortable bars are rare in
small French hotels. There is also a pleasant lobby and
restaurant. The food made no lasting impression, but we
were perfectly content with our stay. The prices at the
Bellevue are a little upmarket – £50 for a double room
with bath and loo and a wide range of menus to choose
from. The cheapest is around £15, ranging to something
much grander at £35. We finished up paying about £60 for
our meal – so it is not particularly cheap.

It is possible to stay at Mâcon without going into the
town at all. On what the French call *l'échangeur* – the exit
to an autoroute – at Mâcon Nord there is a large chain
hotel, the *Novotel*, and 14km North of Mâcon, at an *aire*
off the A6, is another, the *Mercure*. Both these groups are
building more and more hotels right at the edge of autoroutes and very convenient they are for those without much
time and who want comfort and efficiency rather than a
typically French atmosphere. Both have swimming pools
and restaurants; everything such as TVs and direct-dial
phones that one might need is right on the spot. The
Mercure is the more expensive and luxurious, at around
£60 for a double room with bath and all mod cons. The
Novotel is around £15 cheaper.

The only snag with these hotels is that it is unrewarding
to be stuck at the edge of an autoroute and away from the
human life of a village or town. But they do have definite
advantages on occasions when time is running short or
something goes amiss. The time when the *Hôtel Metropole*
gave away my room it was a *Novotel* at Boulogne that
came to my rescue. At 1am the doors were open, there
was a night porter, a spartan room in the modern manner
and an excellent buffet breakfast at an early hour. Being
somewhat impersonal, chain hotels may not always be
what one expects from France, but they do give good
service to the traveller. For this reason one should never
reject staying with them out of hand.

Slightly less expensive than the *Novotel* and *Mercure*
chains are the *Ibis* group hotels. These, too, can often be
found on the outskirts of towns near to the autoroute
échangeur and their restaurants are open till 11.30pm.

All three groups also have hotels in some town centres,
but they seem to us to have less purpose there.

There is an even less expensive chain rapidly mush-rooming in France: the *Formula 1* hotels. These are also mostly close to *échangeurs* and look like funny little dolls' houses with red-painted roofs. They offer rooms for one, two or three people at incredibly low prices – as low as £13 for three people at the time of writing, depending on location.

These are robot hotels, where a machine takes your money and gives you a key. The rooms, not surprisingly, are very small and basic indeed. But when bust on the way home they could prove a godsend.

If robot and chain hotels hold no appeal, you can find yourself a little gem of a halt, the *Relais du Mâconnais*, about 14km from Mâcon. Come off the autoroute at Mâcon Sud, turn left towards the village of Varennes-les-Mâcon and take the little road over the autoroute, and turn right for the village of Charnay. This takes you to the **N79**, direction Cluny and Moulins. The **N79** by-passes the **D17**, where the villages of Berzé-la-

La Croix Blanche

Ville and **La Croix Blanche** are. It is at La Croix that you will find the *Relais du Mâconnais*. To get there, either run straight on to the **D17** at the point where the **N79** bends to form the by-pass, or stay on the **N79**, turning right at the signpost for Berzé-la-Ville and La Croix Blanche.

The *Relais du Mâconnais* is a smart, friendly restaurant hotel run by the chef-proprietor, Christian Lannuel and his wife, Raymonde. They are lavishing both love and money on their hotel. At present there are 12 bedrooms, with more planned. The rooms are not large but comforta-bly appointed, the bathrooms modern and well lit. A night's stay for two costs just under £30.

The restaurant is immaculate and restful, comfortably furnished in warm colours and with white linen and flowers on the tables. The food is both impressive and reasonably priced, with puffy cheese canapés and a tiny taste of fresh salmon mousse served with the aperitifs. For the £13 menu we were served a warm *mousseline* of *foie de volaille*, accompanied by *écrevisse*. Philip's *escargots* were served in a quiche made with a creamy Mâconnais sauce.

We both chose a chicken dish – slices of breast cut in the same fashion as *maigret* of duck and covered with a piquant sauce. It was either cheese or dessert and the sweet trolley won our vote.

The bill, with aperitifs and wine, came to just under £85 for the night – and very good value, too.

Mâcon is roughly 70km from Lyon and it was here that we once began an attempt to find an agreeable way to by-pass Lyon from the North-east. We left the motorway and travelled through the Bresse region of France.

We certainly dodged Lyon, but it was a tedious drive. Bresse is famous for supplying the queen of poultry – a Bresse chicken, often fed on sweetcorn and milk, which makes the bird's skin slightly yellow and the flesh very white. Only chickens from Bresse are entitled to an *Appellation d'Origine Contrôlée* and undoubtedly Bresse chickens are extremely good. The area is also famous for Bleu de Bresse cheeses.

What it is not famous for is scenery.

This attempt at a Lyon by-pass also took rather a long time. We decided it was a straight choice between the possible problems of the busy Lyon autoroute or the boredom of driving through Bresse. Since, with luck, there are occasions when it is possible to breeze through Lyon, we decided to settle for the autoroute. The drive through Bresse is always going to be tedious.

Determined not to be beaten, on another occasion we attempted to by-pass Lyon to the West. That, too, was tedious and complicated and took even longer. We have reluctantly come to accept that unless one does something really dramatic, like taking the old route over the Alps that Napoleon took when he escaped from Elba and landed at Golfe Juan, before setting off for Paris over the mountains, it is best to take the autoroute through Lyon.

Except . . . a new stretch of autoroute is being built around Lyon as I write. It will by-pass the town on the East, starting off with the **A6** below Villefranche and swinging round the town to rejoin the Autoroute du Soleil above Vienne. At present there is no finishing date, but remember to look out for it at any time after the summer of 1993.

Should you find yourself nearing Lyon towards evening, it is better to stop short of the town. Once embarked on crossing Lyon there is no point in not pushing on until you get to Vienne, 40km from the outskirts of Lyon. Apart from the Paris Périphérique, this road through Lyon and down to Vienne is the busiest part of the journey and the most unattractive, though with luck the new autoroute will change all that.

Taking the route through Lyon, one drives past vast petrol refineries, all manner of industry and, though the wide Rhône is a most beautiful river, hereabouts it has been harnessed to man's needs. It is a busy, fast, three-lane highway most of the way to Vienne and the most comfortable spot, until you become immune to the amount of traffic, is the second lane. It is a mistake to try to keep up with the French on this road. In the days when I was younger and bolder and driving in the fast lane a Frenchman once actually overtook my little Mini on the far side. I still can't work out how he did it.

There are, of course, hotels in this industrial sprawl of scruffy towns. The only possible overnight stopping point on the journey is at a *Mercure* hotel which sits isolated at **Chasse-sur-Rhône**, right in the middle of a commercial centre, but once within its doors you are shielded from the surroundings. Things do not perk up until you arrive at Vienne, a lovely old town where the Rhône becomes a proper river again.

But where to stop before Lyon? The capital of Beaujolais, **Villefranche-sur-Saône** in the Grande Vallée du Rhône, is only 31km from Lyon and has an aptly named hotel, the *Plaisance*. We have stayed at this rather smart, well run hotel on several occasions. The only snag is that it is easy to get lost looking for it. The trick is to stick firmly to the **N6** when you leave the autoroute, following the *centre-ville* signs. The **N6** becomes the Boulevard Bernand and the Avenue Libération, where the *Plaisance* is situated, is off the Bernand, near a covered market and a huge *parking*. Coming from the North, look to your left; from the South, to your right. One snag: the Libération is one-way, going the wrong way. You have to drive round the parking area.

The *Plaisance* overlooks the large square, which is mostly used for parking, but there are times of the year when it is taken over by a funfair. Usual advice: ask for a room at the back. It has no restaurant, though there is a well appointed, small and expensive restaurant, *La Fontaine Bleue*, next door to the hotel across from the hotel back door and through the private *parking*. You can eat here off linen table cloths and with suave service for

Chasse-sur-Rhône

Villefranche-sur-Saône

around £12 a head and with half a carafe of wine thrown in. For the style and ambience of the restaurant, it is reasonably priced and the food is not at all bad.

Just around the corner, on the Place Carnot, there is the large, friendly old-fashioned *Brasserie du Rhône*, where you can get a super omelette or steak and little thin French chips with a fresh green salad ridiculously cheaply. We admit to liking it better.

If you don't want the problem of negotiating the town, there is an *Ibis* hotel at the *échangeur* by the Villefranche *péage*. The *Ibis* are simpler than either the *Novotels* or *Mercures*, but perfectly acceptable. This one has 115 rooms, so it is pretty unlikely to be full.

In the morning you should be fresh and ready to face the drive through Lyon – and the earlier you can start, the better.

7

Lyon to Aix-en-Provence

Vienne It was after our successful, but unlikely to be repeated attempt to by-pass Lyon to the East that we neared **Vienne**, at just about the time to stop and settle for the night. Vienne is a fine city stretched along the Rhône, with interesting Roman ruins. But it is busy: one of those places where there is always a problem getting rid of the car. For this reason we have never stayed the night there, preferring to be just outside.

On this occasion we were getting a little anxious, as it was early autumn and, if possible, we like to be settled before 6pm at the latest. We were approaching Vienne on the **D75** from Crémieu and found ourselves at Pont-Evêque, 3km from the centre of Vienne, where the D75 meets the **D502**. Just 6km away to the East on the

Estrablin **D502** there is a country hotel, *La Gabetière*, at **Estrablin** – a village by-passed by the main road and so tiny that if you blink you miss it.

This is a lovely hotel: a 16th-century château where the Protestant Calvin hid for a month when he was in bad odour with the Catholic French. The house is named for another Protestant who lived there, a Monsieur Gabet, who supplied the court of François I with fish and was assassinated for his pains. More recently the mansion was the home of the Marquise de la Valette, from whom the present owner's grandmother bought it. It is set in its own park, furnished much as it was when it was a home, and totally, blissfully peaceful.

133

After driving through the gates and parking in the grounds, one enters the house through an elegant foyer that runs into a big, comfortable drawing room, furnished with great style and taste. There is a tiny bar in the corner and this whole gracious living area is for the use of guests. It is cleverly lit and there is absolutely nothing to suggest that the charming rooms are part of an hotel.

The bedrooms are on the first and second floors, up winding stone stairs and off broad, paved hallways. These rooms are large enough to contain a seating area and a desk and TV. The views are out over the leafy park where, on our first visit, an autumn mist hung in the trees. The furnishings are well loved antiques, but the large bathrooms could not be more modern or tastefully appointed.

It is owned and run by the charming Madame Renée Marcellen, who loves a chat, and her equally friendly daughter, Nicole. When complimented on her beautiful establishment, Madame Renée explained that it had been her childhood home. An only child, she had inherited the house on the death of her parents, but lacking the means to run such a big residence (there are 12 bedrooms and bathrooms), 13 years ago she had turned it into a hotel.

Our bedroom had a distinct atmosphere of times past (perhaps Monsieur Gabet was about) but this comfortable room costs less than £30 for a double. Continental breakfast is less than £3 a head. In Britain it would cost twice as much. We can sincerely recommend this hotel, and on page 181 you will find how to get there from the autoroute.

Vienne   It is an enchanting place to stay, but unfortunately there is no restaurant. Nor is there one nearby. It means a trip to Vienne to eat. This is no problem in the evenings as the streets are clearer and it is possible to park, but it would be difficult at lunchtime. But the drive to Vienne is an interesting one. The road is high, cutting through wooded hills until it drops down a dizzy slope into Vienne.

We ate at the *Restaurant St-Maurice*, in the Place Saint-Maurice, where there are several restaurants to choose from. Place Saint-Maurice is not difficult to find, as it is just back from the *quai* and opposite the suspension bridge.

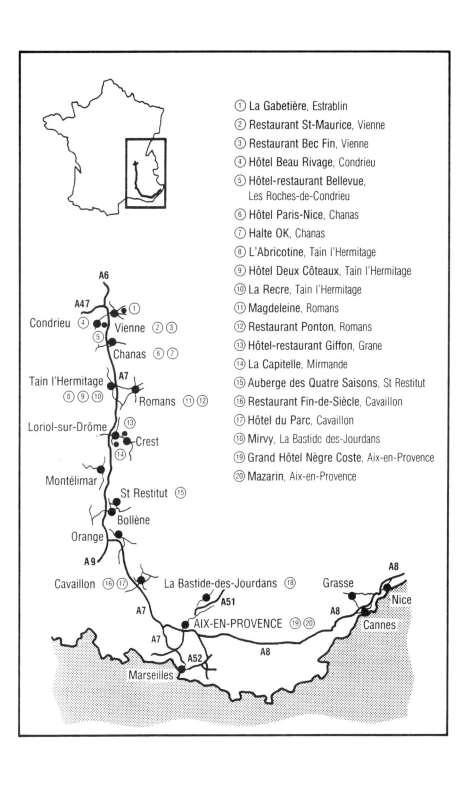

① La Gabetière, Estrablin
② Restaurant St-Maurice, Vienne
③ Restaurant Bec Fin, Vienne
④ Hôtel Beau Rivage, Condrieu
⑤ Hôtel-restaurant Bellevue,
Les Roches-de-Condrieu
⑥ Hôtel Paris-Nice, Chanas
⑦ Halte OK, Chanas
⑧ L'Abricotine, Tain l'Hermitage
⑨ Hôtel Deux Côteaux, Tain l'Hermitage
⑩ La Recre, Tain l'Hermitage
⑪ Magdeleine, Romans
⑫ Restaurant Ponton, Romans
⑬ Hôtel-restaurant Giffon, Grane
⑭ La Capitelle, Mirmande
⑮ Auberge des Quatre Saisons, St Restitut
⑯ Restaurant Fin-de-Siècle, Cavaillon
⑰ Hôtel du Parc, Cavaillon
⑱ Mirvy, La Bastide des-Jourdans
⑲ Grand Hôtel Nègre Coste, Aix-en-Provence
⑳ Mazarin, Aix-en-Provence

A6
A47
Condrieu ④
Vienne ② ③
⑤
Chanas ⑥ ⑦
A7
Tain l'Hermitage
⑧ ⑨ ⑩
Romans ⑪ ⑫
Loriol-sur-Drôme
⑬
Crest
⑭
Montélimar
St Restitut ⑮
Bollène
Orange
A9
Cavaillon ⑯ ⑰
La Bastide-des-Jourdans ⑱
Grasse
A8
A51
A8
Nice
AIX-EN-PROVENCE ⑲ ⑳
Cannes
A7
A7
A8
A52
Marseilles

The best restaurant in this square is the *Bec Fin*, but we decided to experiment with the *St-Maurice*. Unfortunately the meal we had there was not exceptional and we weren't surprised that the small, bright room never filled up. But the staff *almost* made up for the food. They were friendly and chatty, managing to create a good atmosphere in a near-empty restaurant. They were also *gentils*. When a pretty young girl arrived back at her car to find she had a flat, they left to a man, chef included, to fix it for her. And she wasn't even a client.

Though the meal was not a particularly good £20 worth, since the standard was not high (maybe the flat tyre had something to do with that!) we did enjoy ourselves and went back to *La Gabetière* in a cheerful frame of mind.

Condrieu

Les Roches-de-Condrieu

Had it been a little earlier we would have pressed on to the town of **Condrieu**, on the other side of the river, which is a more convenient stopping point. Condrieu houses two exceptional hotels – the *Beau Rivage*, sited on the Rhône, with one Michelin star for food, and the *Bellevue*, also on the river but on the other bank in the tiny little town of **Les Roches-de-Condrieu**. You go over a quaint, old-fashioned iron bridge to get to it. To get to both of them, come off the **A6** at the Condrieu sign, just a few kilometres to the south of Vienne, and follow the signs on the **N86**, a distance of 13km. This area produces some of the best white wine in the Côte du Rhône, but how is something of a mystery. Driving past the vineyards that line the route, you will see that the slopes on which they grow are practically vertical. I often wonder if they are tended by folk wearing climbing boots and using crampons. Nevertheless, the Condrieu whites are exceptional and are made from an unusual grape, the *viognier*, which is the only species allowed to be grown in the area.

The *Beau Rivage* is in Condrieu itself, a little tucked away but well-signposted. It consists of two buildings set back off the road in their own pretty gardens, with a fine big terrace overhanging the Rhône. It is a great pity that during the last decade or so a large factory has been built a short distance down the river. If you sit on the terrace look resolutely to the left: then it will not spoil your view.

But forget the factory. In summer meals are served on

the terrace under the shade of a spreading plane tree, and the *Beau Rivage* has elegant, comfortable bedrooms with bath, most of which are in the annexe. It is the kind of hotel where great big white fluffy bathrobes are supplied to fit even the most rotund. The main hotel building houses a small but smart reception area with a rather *chic* bar beyond. The restaurant is truly classy, as is the cuisine. But the trouble with class is that it comes at a price. The best double here is over £80 for the night, and the most reasonable menu is just under £30 a head, without wine. If you go for the works, counting a little something with the compliments of the chef and a sorbet in the middle, seven courses are served. Expect to pay £40 a head without wine for this kind of treat. If you can stretch to it, and if you can get in, stay here. The staff are professional and charming. It is one of those 'your wish is our command' places. But because of this, it does get heavily booked. If your heart is set on spending a night at the *Beau Rivage*, do reserve well in advance.

Even if the *Beau Rivage* is too expensive or you can't get in, no-one could be disappointed with the *Bellevue*. It *is* a *belle vue*, actually prettier than the *Beau Rivage*, since the once rather scruffy river frontage has been turned into a jolly little marina. For years now the same rather stern, elderly proprietor, Monsieur Bouron, has been sitting at the desk as one enters the hotel, solemnly checking his bookings and dispensing rooms. I'm always worried he won't be there next time. There is a large breakfast room which is also used as a bar and a small but comfortable lounge with lots of magazines lying about. The rooms are not grand, but they are comfortable, and the nicest and quietest are those overlooking the river. They cost around £30 for a double with bath.

The restaurant is large, again overlooking the river, and the standard of food is high, with the cheapest menu at about £12 a head without wine. I have never had a bad meal there. The *Bellevue* does not have the glamour of its neighbour over the river, nor is it as expensive. In many ways I like it better: familiarity, perhaps, as I have stayed there so many times; at first when I couldn't get into the *Beau Rivage*, and later on its own merits. Also, at Les Roches-de-Condrieu, you can wander along the river, inspecting the boats in the new marina and working up an appetite for dinner. Walking is not so easy in Condrieu itself.

Whichever hotel you choose, start your journey the next morning by breezing down the right bank of the Rhône on the **N86**, and marvel at those impossible vineyards. Cross the river at Sablons to Chanas, 23km from Condrieu, over a surprisingly long bridge. It's no distance and is well signposted to the autoroute.

Chanas

In the May of 1991, when we were coming back from a cold, wet fortnight in Les Eygages, we reached **Chanas** around lunchtime, and, never having been into the town, decided to check it out. It proved to be one of those Marie-Celeste-style French places where no-one is about and nothing is happening, though it must come to life at some time, since there is a huge open space to house a fruit market. Chanas village has no cafés, no restaurants, no life. We finished up having lunch at *Paris-Nice*, a nice little two-storey, red-roofed hotel on the **N7**, two minutes from the Chanas autoroute exit and right opposite a great spaghetti mass of railway lines which might have been the marshalling yards. The hotel is *insonorisé* – soundproofed – and has private parking; the rooms have TVs and only cost just over £25 with bath and £21 with shower.

The restaurant is cosy and cheerful, with red decoration and lots of well polished wood. But they threw us. We had decided to eat lightly and asked for some pâté followed by an omelette. The helping of pâté was delicious, but enormous. The omelettes must each have contained four eggs and came with three large helpings of vegetables and Lyonnaise potatoes. We were given a slice of rather sweet *tarte maison* to follow. The food was hardly delicate, but would have been appreciated by anyone young and hungry and hard-up. With a bottle of Côte du Rhône and coffee, it all came to £20.

At the Chanas *échangeur* is a hotel called the *Halte OK*. It has yellow stuccoed walls rising for five floors above the flat countryside. You can hardly miss it. Somehow, we've never fancied the place, but for our neighbours, Dick and Kath, it was a port in a storm. They had headed for Les Roches-de-Condrieu and found the *Bellevue* closed, and rushed back to the *Beau Rivage* in Condrieu, who had no room. As they had driven from Calais that morning it was something of a disaster to find themselves driving in the dark and looking for an hotel. In desperation they headed back to the autoroute at Chanas. Dick was beginning to think that they would have to spend the night in the car when Kath let out a yelp. 'An hotel!' she cried.

Sure enough, like a beacon shone the garish, tasteless but oh, so wonderful word H O T E L in huge green neon letters along the top of a roof. And as the road swung round, the equally brilliantly lit name, *Halte OK*, on the side wall came into view.

Dick said it sounded like some place in the Wild West, but at that point he wouldn't have cared if it had been a home for abandoned French dogs, as long as there was a bed up for the night.

There was. Inside the hotel was cheerful and brightly lit – most unusual for an inexpensive French hotel. The rooms, costing under £30 for a double, are shoe-box style but with a well appointed bathroom. Clean, pleasant but characterless was how Kath described it.

The hotel has the lively *Trattoria di Righi* attached, which serves good pastas at a reasonable price, as well as some French food. It proved to be a useful and comfortable resting place.

The trouble with stopping at Chanas is that all the accommodation is on the main road or the *échangeur*. There is nowhere to wander and views of the marshalling yards or the autoroute don't exactly rest the eye.

Tain l'Hermitage

Better to push on if there is time, perhaps to **Tain l'Hermitage**. We once came off the autoroute here just for breakfast at a small hotel, *L'Abricotine*, 4km along the route to Romans and right in the country. I fell in love with the *Abricotine*. It stood four-square, a sturdy little building in a garden full of sunflowers. The entrance was small and the restaurant where we ate our excellent croissants and drank good strong coffee had such a pleasant atmosphere that I wished we were staying.

We have always intended to go back, but circumstances have never quite permitted it. There was an occasion when it would have been possible, when we arrived rather late in Tain l'Hermitage one autumn. It was just getting dark, and we were anxious that a hotel as small as *L'Abricotine* (it has only 10 rooms) would be fully booked. We settled for staying in the town.

But we must warn you that Tain is a gastronomic

desert. Our hotel, the *Deux Côteaux*, was most pleasant and run by a friendly couple, Françoise and Denis Voillemin, and their welcoming dog, whose rôle appeared to be to greet all arrivals and then go back to sleep again. For under £30 our room was pleasantly furnished with slightly battered antiques, but had long windows that opened on to a wrought-iron balcony looking down over the *quai* and the river. What it did not have was a restaurant.

We went searching for one. The *Reynaud*, the Michelin-recommended eating place, was closed. The narrow main street was unpleasant to walk, with vast juggernauts thundering by. This is unusual in a town so near the autoroute, and as we weren't aware of any roadworks or diversions on the **A7** we couldn't understand why the traffic was so unpleasantly heavy.

In the end we settled for a *crêperie*, *La Recre*, in the Place du Taurobole, which was at least away from the noise of the juggernauts. We were pleasantly surprised. *La Recre* is a bright and cheerful little café run by an efficient young woman with a lovely smile. We did not have to eat crêpes – I had a *steak au poivre* and my husband had – you've guessed it – an omelette. We both had those irresistible chips, all washed down with a bottle of Crozes Hermitage. With coffee, salads, a slice of lemon tart and another glass of wine for Philip, it cost us £9 a head.

If you tire of autoroute driving, Tain is a good place to come off, as there is a beautiful country drive to enjoy and one that doesn't take that long: the road is quiet and reasonably straight. This road cuts out Valence and you can either get back on the **A6** at Loriol or continue, on a slightly more complicated route, rejoining the autoroute past Montélimar. The exact details are on page 181.

Beginning the diversion, leave the autoroute at **Romans** Tain/Tournon and take the **D532** to **Romans**, a good-sized town in the Drôme, famous for the manufacture of shoes. We did once stay here but had the impression it was not really geared for tourism. It is a handsome rather than elegant town, with a couple of recommended hotels, the *Cendrillon* and the *Magdeleine*, which have nothing to choose between them. They are reasonable at about £25 for a double with bath or shower.

After having booked into the *Magdeleine* we set off looking for a meal and walked through the town to the *Ponton* restaurant in the Place Jacquemart, again Michelin-recommended. It was extraordinary. The town was deserted. There was no-one on the streets, no sign of life anywhere. The cafés were empty – there seemed to be no-one to guide us. Fortunately we found the rather splendid Place Jacquemart, with its fine clock tower dating from the 14th century, on our own. We admired it with no traffic, no people in an empty square. The restaurant was empty, too. We ate in solitary silence, wondering about this unfortunate town which had to be going through the worst recession in history.

It seemed particularly unfair on the pretty restaurant, set in a high-ceilinged room with wide doors that opened to the silent street. The food, *nouvelle cuisine*, was excellent – and yet we were the only clients.

We paid our reasonable bill and left, walking through the eerily quiet streets before stopping at a large café on a roundabout to order a nightcap, since our hotel had no restaurant. The waiters had only half-a-dozen people to serve.

Then suddenly all hell broke loose. It began with the hooting of cars and shouts, and then what seemed like dozens of cars, dangerously full of people, hanging out of windows, clinging to the roofs, all bawling their heads off and punching the horn as they went in dangerous convoy round and round the roundabout. The din was indescribable.

The waiter bringing our drinks had a grin that split his face in half.

'What is it?' we asked. 'What has happened?'

'France,' he said, putting down his tray with a flourish, 'has won *le football*.'

You'd have thought they'd won the Third World War. The din went on all night until the early hours. Every street was packed with marauding motor-cars. No-one in Romans could have had any sleep – including us.

In the morning we set off on our beautiful drive down the **D538** to Chabeuil and Crest, a distance of 36km. It's a straight, easy road, through fields of sunflowers, lavender, cattle; generally agricultural and very quiet, with the mountains hovering in rings around. The driving is easy and cuts out the race-track of the **A6** around Valence, where the road curves along the side of the river. In the last few years this river-stretch of the autoroute has been much improved, but driving through the villages and the sunflowers is less nerve-wracking.

Crest

Crest is a pretty little town on the Drôme river and from here it is easy to get to another of our favourite places, the *Giffon* at **Grane**. This is recommended both for lunch and an overnight stop. Going South, cross the river in Crest and on the edge of the town turn right on to the **D104**, signposted Loriol. In about 7km you will arrive in the small town of Grane. Should you be coming from the autoroute, leave by the Loriol exit and take the Crest

Grane

road until you reach Grane. The *Giffon* is in the middle of the main street, next to a church – an uncompromising little hotel, flat-fronted and shuttered with a small court-yard at the side.

Philip always refers to this hotel as 'cathedral calm'. Out of season one eats in the indoor restaurant, a peaceful room with high-backed striped chairs, white linen and fresh flowers. The room is curiously quiet, but not with that embarrassing quietness with everyone speaking in whispers. It just seems to mop up sound. In summer, one eats in the cool of the little courtyard – and one eats very well, though expect to pay about £18 a head, with wine for the cheapest menu.

The rooms are simple. The *Giffon* is all about food and is basically a restaurant. There are only nine rooms, costing under £25 for a double with bath. It is a family concern, run by Patric Giffon since his father retired a few years ago. It is a pleasant place to stay, as there are pretty walks and little traffic. This is a delightful, quiet stopping place, especially in the summer, when there is enough light to explore. A tiny river runs close by with an arched stone bridge – a favourite spot for small boys to fish.

The *Giffon* is only 10km off the autoroute, Loriol *échangeur*, or you can go back to Crest and take the rest of the country road to below Montélimar, as described on page 181.

This part of the route is slower driving, as the road winds over foothills that offer stunning views of the Alps to the East. There is little traffic so not much hassle, though picking up the autoroute is a touch complicated.

Mirmande

On this road one by-passes the hotel *Capitelle* at **Mirmande**, described in our **Autumn Journey** chapter. As much as we like the *Giffon*, the *Capitelle* is perhaps more interesting, and, of course, more expensive. And the village of Mirmande is more picturesque than the down-to-earth Grane.

St Restitut

Though Mirmande is peaceful there is a sense of life and purpose about the village. Another village where we once stayed, **St Restitut** – only 9km away from Bollène, still going further South and just off the autoroute – is a similar Drôme village set on a peak as protection from the invaders of the Middle Ages, when this part of France struggled through endless religious wars. St Restitut, however, is almost creepily quiet, another village with a definite touch of the Marie-Celestes. No-one seemed to be home when we arrived there. We did find a rather gloomy and not very clean bar for a pre-dinner drink, but there were only three other customers, obviously all regulars and they didn't seem particularly pleased to see us.

Two ancient churches crown the village, and the *Auberge des Quatre Saisons* hotel, where we stayed, sits behind them. That, too, was quaint. Our bedroom, costing around £45 with bath, was crammed full of old, though not unpleasant furniture, but we couldn't make out why there was a sideboard instead of a chest of drawers or a dressing table. The room gave the impression that the hotel owner had moved house – to somewhere smaller – and was determined to cram in every last bit of furniture that he or she owned. But then, the hotel was an old *mas* and must have been a superb private home at some time in its past.

The restaurant was across the road in another *mas* opposite, and that was charming. A pretty room, made from an ancient *cave* with a great curved door into the street. It was cleverly lit to warm the stone walls and served extremely good food. The portions were generous. It even had diners who had sprung from somewhere in this silent village. The cheapest menu is around £15, but there is a five-course meal at around £20 a head. French restaurants like to develop their own little individual touches. At the *Quatre Saisons* it was the sugar. When the coffee arrived, the waitress's knees were fairly buckling under the weight of not a sugar bowl, but a sugar tray. On it were dishes of every kind and colour of sugar, including large lumps of solid sugar which were surprisingly heavy. Unfortunately this was all rather wasted on me. I don't take sugar.

Pleasant as the restaurant was, taking into account that Mirmande and St Restitut are both in the Drôme and are both hilltop villages, we would pick Mirmande every time, but you won't be disappointed if fate throws you off the autoroute at Bollène and you settle for the *Quatre Saisons*.

To retrace our steps a little to Montélimar Sud, here one might as well take the autoroute, as it is rather shorter than the old **N7** and also because the views are, if not beautiful, interesting. It is a strange road between Montélimar and Pont-St-Esprit: another of those areas where the Rhône has been sacrificed to man's needs. All along the river are vast hydro-electric plants and factories and, most notably, at Donzère-Mondragon, the great towers of the Tricastin nuclear atomic plant belonging to the French electricity board – the EDF. You can see the great pillars of white smoke rising from these two towers for miles. Donzère-Mondragon sounds more like a place in *The Lord of the Rings* than a huge nuclear plant, but it would be unfair to say that these works are ugly. They are dramatic, almost grand against the mountains. And it also seems odd that Tricastin produces rather good wine, in spite of the industrialisation of the river that presumably irrigates the vineyards.

Going South not long after Mondragon, one sees on the rocky cliffs that line the road the battered remains of the ancient fortress of Mornas. This tumbled craggy edifice, now like broken teeth, must in its time have had equal strength to its modern neighbours across the river.

Only 10kms to Orange now, the spot where the Autoroute du Soleil parts, with one sprig going off to Spain through the Languedoc and South-west France. The road to the Côte d'Azur becomes two lanes here, but the traffic lessens, and there is a different feel in the air. The earth begins to look ruddier, the sky blue-er and there's a warmth and softness in the air. This is Provence and we head for dusty, timeless **Cavaillon**, a town we like so much that we always try to find a reason to pop in. This is not difficult, as it couldn't be closer to the autoroute, making a great excuse for stopping for

Cavaillon

coffee, or lunch, or tea or indeed, the night.

Cross the Durance, a wide, slow-flowing river: Cavaillon is just on the other side and seems to come to a sudden finish when it bumps up against a miniature mountain. The town is not large, but is awash with restaurants and little bars. Since Cavaillon produces the best melons in all France as well as wonderful asparagus, cherries, strawberries, peaches and apricots it is an important market town and full of Southern life. We have never stayed here more than one night at a time, but it would be a good jumping-off point for exploring this part of Provence, as it is only 20km from Avignon, 40km from Orange and close to the Carmargue.

If we stop by just for breakfast or a drink, we park in the Place du Clos right at the end of the town, where there is a particularly handsome big, old fin-de-siècle bar, with marble tables, mirrors and old murals, and wide doors opening on to the street. It's a bit scruffy, with odd piles of vegetables and cases of wine shoved in corners, but in its day it must have been glorious. Above this is a rather smart restaurant under different management, called, would you believe, *La-Fin-de-Siècle*, where in elegant surroundings *nouvelle cuisine* is served along with a mixture of traditional dishes. Also at this far end of the town, where the green miniature mountain stands guard, is the *Hôtel du Parc* where we like to stay. Set on the Place François Tourel, this is a nice old dignified hotel with a fountain in the inner courtyard. There is no restaurant, but there is a tiny breakfast room. We had a very happy stay in this hotel. Our room had a big solid wardrobe, a good bed and long windows. Madame Lancelot, who greeted us, was friendly and charming, and recommended us to dine at the *Fin-de-Siècle*, just across the road.

There are some excellent shops in the town, particularly those dealing in food and wine, but it is the general ambience of the place that is so pleasing. It's attractive, warm both climatically and personally, and you just know from the feeling of the air and the look of the skies that you are in the South.

A very pleasant detour can be taken from Cavaillon through the Luberon mountains. Quite honestly this detour will save no time – quite the reverse – but for a look at a different part of Provence it is an easy drive;

there is a charming hotel at the end of it and a 30-minute run back to the autoroute at Aix-en-Provence in the morning. If you are bored with autoroute driving, or simply frazzled by it, this road cuts out 47km of the **A7**, but gives you around 100km of country road driving instead.

La Bastide-des-Jourdans

We think it is worth it for the pleasure of staying at the *Mirvy* hotel in **La Bastide-des-Jourdans**, up in the Luberon mountains. At first the road skirts the mountains but when at Pertuis – quite an important little Provence town – the road begins to climb up towards the Luberon Parc National, it becomes more interesting and one drives through enchanting little rocky villages before coming to La Bastide-des-Jourdans.

Drive right through the little town and out the other side, then keep your eyes peeled to the left, as the *Mirvy* is quite high off the road. This, of course, gives it the most wonderful view across a wide expanse of mountains, and all the 10 bedrooms, built a few paces away from the main hotel, face out through terrace windows on to this exceptional view. It was pelting with rain the night we first stayed there. I had to run from the annexe to the restaurant with an improvised raincoat made from a plastic dry-cleaning bag over my head and the young waitress had difficulty hiding her giggles.

The hotel is run by Mireille Abello, an attractive young woman who exudes an air of calm. Everything is done in a gentle, easy-going manner and with style. She showed us to our room, stood and waited to test the temperature and then said we would want the heating on. Even though it was late April and that far South, the weather was not clement and we were pleased when she switched on a radiator. The big, airy room soon warmed up and we made ourselves at home. Comfortably furnished with a desk and chair as well as the usual bedroom furniture, the place was cosy and the bathroom quite exotic – all tiles and mod cons, though we had a modern, efficient shower rather than a bath. We felt the accommodation was fairly priced at £50 a double for the night.

The *Mirvy* is set in large, well cared-for grounds right in the middle of the national park. There is a good-sized swimming pool – though on our visit in that early spring, it was quite wet enough outside without getting wetter swimming. Each bedroom has its own terrace, facing

South. The entrance to the annexe where the bedrooms are is most elegant, with local wine, honey and some handicrafts on sale, but the stone house where the restaurant is situated is the heart of this hotel.

With stone floors, Victorian lamps, lace tablecloths and rustic chairs and a big open fire which was blazing away on our visit, this restaurant is more than a bit special. There are three excellent menus as well as an *à la carte*. The least expensive, *'menu de tradition'*, is around £15; the *'menu de la mer'* is about £17 and the *'menu degustation'* costs £40 for seven courses.

We can never seem to manage seven courses, apart from the fact that £80 before you've so much as ordered a bottle of mineral water is a bit steep unless it's a special occasion. Neither of us fancied fish, so we settled for the £15 menu. For this I had a delicious salad of lambs' tongues and brains, while Philip chose the duck and orange pâté. We both had an escalope of veal, finishing with cheese and dessert. The puddings were excellent home-made tarts. With a bottle of St Estèphe, a Beaumes de Venise (a local sweet wine which I like to drink with dessert), the meal cost under £50.

We were intrigued with the *Mirvy*'s list of aperitifs, alcohols and liqueurs of Provence, some of which we had never encountered before. They are specialities of the *maison*. There was a *bau des muscats-frizzant*, a sweetish, fruity, lightly sparkling wine which you could drink either with dessert or throughout the meal. *Rinquinquin à la pêche*, an aperitif, made with seven varieties of peaches in good white wine, and with a touch of vanilla and nuts for good measure, cost around £2 and, for the same price, green nuts with muscat grapes and cinnamon are blended to make the *Noix de la St-Jean*. This aperitif was created to complement the melons of Cavaillon or to drink with dessert. A liqueur, *La Farigole*, made with a base of thyme, ends the meal on a perfumed note.

Madame Abello created the hotel herself eight years ago, when she had it specially built. Young as the buildings are, they have weathered and mellowed under the Provence sun and one would believe they had been there for generations. Madame runs the hotel alone and efficiently. It is a lovely place to visit.

On the morning after our stay at the *Mirvy*, the landscape was shrouded in thick, white mist but the rain had miraculously vanished. By the time we had dropped down from the *alpilles* (foothills) the sun was shining as we drove round Aix-en-Provence. From here it is roughly 150km and an hour-and-a-half's drive to Cannes. The journey is virtually over. Unless, of course, you fancy spending some time in Aix-en-Provence . . .

Aix-en-Provence

Aix-en-Provence, like Paris and Beaune, deserves a special visit. It is a seductive old town, terracotta in colour, with a profusion of magnificent fountains, fine buildings, wide avenues lined with old, gnarled plane trees and, because of its University, full of young life.

Perhaps because it is the capital of Provence, something always seems to be going on in Aix. I once arrived there in April not realising that it was the night of their carnival. This was a remarkable stroke of luck, as the carnival can happen either in March or April and does not have a fixed date. If one really wanted to see it, advance planning and a phone call to the French Tourist Office in London or the Aix-en-Provence Tourist Office would be necessary. It could prove quicker to ring Aix, given the time the French Tourist Office takes to answer the phone!

The carnival makes its way down to the heart of the town, the beautiful and broad Cours Mirabeau. The wide pavement is barricaded off as the procession goes by. To watch it is a fascinating, not altogether comfortable experience. The vast and grotesque papier-mâché figures, swaying as high as the trees and brilliantly lit by the street lamps, have a pagan fascination. Most of these figures are ugly – giants, dwarfs, over-endowed women, figures with huge animal heads – and have a sinister air. Then, just as one begins to feel like crossing oneself, along comes a float full of lovely Southern girls flinging flowers to the spectators, escorted by dashing young men on horseback. Then another float, carrying enchanting children in long frilly dresses with flower head-dresses. The procession goes on and on; a mixture of the good and the bad in human nature.

The atmosphere in the town is electric and awash with confetti, as students fling these brightly coloured circles of paper from huge paper bags. If you are unwise enough to open your mouth when one of these young men is near, you will receive a mouthful of the stuff.

It was a spectacular carnival, perhaps not so different from many others, except that the special atmosphere of the town itself adds the final magic.

The last time we went to Aix, we had decided to stay at the *Nègre Coste* hotel on the Cours Mirabeau, so as to be in the centre of things. Again something unexpected was happening. A craft fair had taken over the Cours Mirabeau, taking up the full length of one pavement and one side of the broad avenue. Traffic was at a standstill.

Aix is impossible for parking at the best of times and we had chosen the *Nègre Coste* because it has its own car park. By staying there we would not have to drive around for hours looking for somewhere to leave the car. Leaving Phil double-parked, I rushed into the hotel to see if there was a room. There was, but alas (the charming young girl behind the desk was desolate), the magnetic key to the garage would not work. We would have to use the public *parking*. The best laid schemes . . .

The public *parking*, should you ever need it, is just off a roundabout that curves round the spectacular fountain at the foot of the Cours Mirabeau. Pass the brightly coloured children's roundabout and turn right at the side of the post office. It is well signposted.

We queued for a while to get in and then wandered back in Southern heat to the *Nègre Coste*, an elegant 18th-century residence that has been entirely restored. Our room had a soaring ceiling and was furnished with that pot-bellied French furniture of the period. Long windows, double-glazed, looked out on to the life of the Cours Mirabeau. Even the bed was Louis XV – but, luckily, not the mattress. The TV and mini-fridge did look rather out of place among the moire silk-covered walls, but we pounced on the cold drinks inside – no alcohol apart from one bottle of beer provided.

Our bathroom was smart, tiled and modern and for once with adequate towels – French hotels can be mean with towels and if you plan to stay at really inexpensive establishments you'd better travel with your own.

The building itself was very fine, with a magnificent staircase and a pretty French provincial salon downstairs. Most of the furnishings were from the 18th century, including some lovely Oriental rugs, and we decided that even without the use of their garage, this was a pleasant place to stay.

The craft fair was a bonus, with stall after stall of lovingly made and presented *objets d'art*. We fell in love with the painted wooden toys and ornaments for children: cheerful mobiles of rocking sea-horses, old-fashioned jack-in-the-boxes, spinning tops, egg-cups with clown's faces. All were made by a modest, thin young man whose face lit up when we told him how charming his work was. Everything from furniture to silk screen-printed scarves, paintings, pottery and embroidery was on sale, and nothing we saw was tacky.

Even without the fair, so much was going on. A girl with a white-painted face selling roses. Two boys carrying outsized home-made guitars, square in shape and appearing to be made of ply-wood. Another lad playing statues and standing dead still, his cap at his feet ready for donations. All kinds of *avant garde* street theatre and, in a café, a waiter putting up a parasol and tying a great bunch of balloons on the top of it.

Aix has a certain lightness and gaiety. It is full of smartly dressed people, young and old, who cheerfully eat ice-cream cornets as they walk along the Mirabeau. In a word, it's fun. It's also full of restaurants and cafés, dozens of them, and in our experience they are all pretty much of a muchness. If you arrive there for lunch it makes sense to choose one of the simple cafés, where you will eat a perfectly reasonable meal at a sensible price.

We have had some disappointing dinners in Aix, and this time we planned to try the one restaurant in the town that has a Michelin star. By the time we had got rid of the car and got back to the hotel it was well gone 7pm and the *Clos de la Violette* on the Avenue Violette was sorry, but had no room. So we decided that, since it was Saturday night and the town was buzzing, with the world wandering up and down the Cours Mirabeau, we would try *Le Mazarin*, a big restaurant whose outside tables spill over the Cours itself. We would eat and watch the pageant.

The pageant spilled over into the restaurant; there was never a dull moment. A baby crow somehow managed to join the diners, hiding under the linen tablecloths while a waiter scuffled round the diners' feet to find the bird. As the poor thing was borne off squawking to the back of the restaurant, Philip muttered, 'I hope they're not going to put him in the stock pot.'

In fact, on enquiry, he had been put in a box and was being fed. Lucky crow. The food at the *Mazarin* is good, if a little expensive, but to some extent one pays here for the ambience. It is a beautiful Belle Epoque room with murals on the ceiling and mirrors on the walls and with lots of shining, polished wood. It is also the best seat in the house for watching the animated life of Aix go by.

The restaurant itself was busy with waiters flambé-ing bananas, and bringing in a vast dish, shaped like a gondola, which proved to be a fish *en croûte* (in pastry). We were marvelling at the size of it, since it was being served to only two people, when the man dining alone next to us turned and whispered: 'It's all *croûte*.' And he was right. There wasn't that much fish as the pastry was stripped away.

The speciality is sea-food, and that is what we ate. *Moules marinière* for me, fish soup with all the goodies, croûtons, garlic sauce and grated *gruyère* for Philip. We both had *panachés* of different white fish with prawns for decoration, served on huge plates in very *nouvelle cuisine* fashion; in other words, not much in the way of vegetables. Blackcurrent sorbet for me and lemon tart for Philip completed a meal which cost £75 with aperitifs, a bottle of good white wine and no coffee. We got tired of waiting for that after 27 minutes – and getting the bill took another quarter of an hour.

The *Mazarin* is an experience for the surroundings, though the restaurant is slightly spoilt by an eccentric staff. The bearded head-waiter was wearing a suit that must have been two full sizes too big for him. Our waiter was decidedly grumpy. But then, they were busy, it was Saturday night, and Aix was buzzing. Maybe on a quieter night the service would have been better.

We paid our £55 hotel bill on the following morning and left Aix as the artisans were putting up their stalls for another day's trading. It was a lovely morning, and the town was sparkling in the sunshine. We retrieved our car from the *parking* and had set off on the last stage of our journey when Philip said, 'There's something wrong with the car.'

There was. A puncture. We pulled into a parking area,

luckily deserted so early in the morning, and set about emptying the boot. As Philip wrestled with the wheel, a very small man in striped trousers and a splashy shirt appeared, holding his little daughter by the hand. He seemed fascinated by what was going on. He and the child stood silent, riveted, just watching as the damaged wheel came off until Philip began to try to balance the new one into place. At this point our audience let go of his daughter, squatted on the ground, put the wheel on his lap and held it against the screw holes, while Philip put back the screws. All still without a word. The man then stood up, retrieved his daughter and went back to supervising as the screws were tightened and the punctured tyre put back in the boot. When all was finished, he nodded, as if satisfied at a job well done, and disappeared in the direction of wherever he had been going in the first place, his shy daughter the richer by 50 francs for sweeties.

We were right outside an attractive looking hotel called the *Résidence Rotonde* and Philip popped in to ask if he might wash his hands. 'Of course,' said the manager, in perfect English, and led him to the toilets.

It was not to be. The plumbers were in and the water was off; the manager was desolate. We had to make do with Kleenex and water from the windscreen wipers; a method that proved extremely effective.

At just after 8am we were on our way, Les Eygages and the Côte d'Azur waiting just an hour-and-a-half's drive away.

8

The Côte d'Azur

Let Le Train take the Strain

It is not obligatory to drive to the Côte d'Azur. You can fly to Nice and get a bus or taxi – a helicopter if you feel like it – to your destination; or use the fly-drive system, picking up a pre-hired car at the airport. These arrangements are best made with a good travel agent, since flights to Nice are rarely cheap, but deals can be done. The most important thing to remember if taking a fly-drive or hiring a car in France is to pay for the car in Britain. Pay in France and the hirer is stuck with the French taxes on car-hire, which are astronomic.

Booking in Britain, it is also possible to go by train and have a hired car waiting at one of over 200 French railway stations; you can drop the vehicle off at another station when you leave. Talk to your travel agent for the fine details.

Alternatively, and most luxuriously, it is possible to go by rail overnight and take the car on the train with you – something Philip and I often did in the days when time was short. It is a pleasant way to travel and there is a Calais/Nice, Nice/Calais service every night of the year. This is expensive, though careful sums, adding the cost of the autoroutes, meals on the journey and at least one night in an hotel, make the price seem less alarming. Even so, at the time of writing you should allow for over £700 for two people and a car (according to season) with a T2 sleeper – a comfortable compartment for two – from Calais to Nice return.

There are variations on the theme. It is also possible to book a *couchette* – a bunk with a blanket and a pillow in a cabin for six people. Perfect if there are six of you, or at least if you outnumber the opposition; less attractive if you are travelling alone. That cuts the cost, though not by as much as you might think. It is transporting the car that is expensive. Also, in the years I did it, when much younger, I had some adventures I could have done without.

Some people take the train for only part of the journey. You can board, plus car, at Boulogne and disembark at Avignon, leaving only a morning's drive – and a beautiful drive at that – to the Côte d'Azur. Or, again starting at Boulogne, go a little further to Fréjus-St Raphael (on certain days) and drive the Esterel Corniche to Cannes. This is a spectacular, cliff-hugging climb well worth doing. The views of the coast are wonderful, and the drive itself is not too hairy.

If neither Calais nor Boulogne is a convenient starting place, a drive to Paris gives a great many more possibilities. From Paris the sleeper-car services go to Avignon, Fréjus-St Raphael, Lyon, Marseille, Toulon and Nice – all ports of call on the route to Provence – but they do not necessarily run every day.

If you buy a through ticket with French Railways from Britain there is a concession on the Channel Sealink crossing, so it makes sense to let them complete the booking. For passengers without a car, there is a Sealink crossing which connects with the train that leaves Calais Maritime station spot on 7.40pm, but with the car you need to be there earlier – any time between 5.30 and 6.30pm to have your car loaded. Any later and your car is liable to be left behind, as the car transporter will be out of the loading sidings and chugging away to be attached to the night sleeper.

One snag is that, as Calais Maritime is some distance from the town centre, once you have checked in your car for loading you are either stuck at the station or facing a long walk back to civilisation. On a good day, the rather scruffy station bar with its quite ghastly floppy turquoise plastic table-coverings is open for drinks and snacks. Out of season it is usually firmly shut. We have not managed to conquer this problem. Sometimes we arrive in Calais early in the day and have a slap-up lunch; on other occasions we leave it as late as possible to cross the channel before delivering the car. Either way nothing can prevent that boring hour-and-10-minute wait for the train to leave. The good news is that it is rare for this train not to run on time.

It is all much more fun coming back. At Nice you must leave your car by 5.30pm at the latest. The point of departure is easy to find. Look for the *SNCF* signs to lead you to the station on the Avenue Thiers and then the *autos accompagnées* directions at the side of the station, right in the centre of town. The entrance is next to the new Hotel Arcade and opposite the brick main post office. Having handed your vehicle over to the care of French Railways you can have a trot around the town, do a bit of last-minute shopping or drop into a tea-room or brasserie and watch the world go by. You can even visit the *Flunch* self-service restaurant at the station itself, which is like no station buffet in Britain. It serves good food.

Those travelling *trains autos accompagnées* have a special place to leave baggage, free. This is in the public Left Luggage area at the end of Nice station: on production of your tickets the baggage is specially stored. Being able to get rid of your overnight bag makes it a perfectly reasonable thing to spend the day or an afternoon in Nice, just as long as you get back to the station before the train leaves at 6.40pm.

At both Calais or Nice your car will be inspected for any scratches or damage – just in case anyone should be tempted to blame French Railways for old wounds. Insurance cover against damage is not expensive. You will be handed vouchers for breakfast, included in the price of the tickets. Then your car keys are handed over to a member of the railway staff. He drives your car on to the transporter and seals the car door handle.

On the train, the conductor settles you in and takes away your tickets and your breakfast vouchers. Do not panic. He will return the tickets in the morning, usually during breakfast. When he checks your tickets, this is a good moment to tip him (£5 is OK) in case you want anything during the night. In his little cubby hole at the end of the carriage he keeps a supply of bottled water, alcoholic drinks, a cork-screw and a collection of odd things a passenger might need. He will also serve you an airline-type meal, if you wish. These cost between £9 and £12 without wine and there is a small *à la carte* menu as well, including a piece of *foie gras* for £5.

We prefer to take our own picnic, buying it in France. We have chilled bottles of wine and mineral water in a cold bag (don't forget the corkscrew!) and the fun of this journey is to sit in your own little compartment watching the scenery go by, eating lovely ham, or maybe a lobster or prawns – any favourite food as long as it is cold. The conductor will take away the debris. It really is a bit of an adventure, and though we have travelled this way dozens of times the pleasure has never gone out of it.

We can recommend the T2 wagon-lits. They are second-class, but you would never know it. They have two cleverly arranged and extremely comfortable berths, a little washbasin, and all sorts of nooks and crannies into which luggage can be tucked. There are two different designs of compartment – one with high berths across from each other, and the other with two berths one above the other. These two different designs slot into each other jigsaw fashion in a way I can never quite work out, except to appreciate that the design is brilliantly space-saving. If one of you, however, is a bit creaky on the pins it is as well to request a cabin with one lower berth, to avoid ladder-climbing.

Unfortunately, these compartments do get rather hot. The ventilation system is decidedly iffy, and come bed-time it is a straight choice between roasting or opening the window and putting up with the noise. We settle for the noise. It is about the only occasion on which either of us ever takes a sleeping pill, so noise becomes immaterial. So much so that on one occasion when we woke in the morning we were rather surprised to find our clothing, neatly folded under the window, soaking wet. At some time in the night we had sped through quite a serious thunderstorm.

If you like trains, as we do, this journey is great fun. You pull into Nice at 10.39 in the morning (Calais 9.46, though this can vary) having been served a pleasant continental breakfast. Be prepared for a little wait while your car is unloaded. There is always a sense of relief, similar to spotting your luggage coming round on the carousel at an airport, when you see your car being driven off for you. But in our experience they have never lost one yet.

It is an interesting journey. The scenery, when it is light, is spectacular, particularly when the train is running along the Mediterranean. And there is a club-like atmosphere in the carriages. Many of the passengers are British and, while hanging about the corridor to keep cool before going to bed, get chatting. Sitting in our little compartment and scoffing our picnic we have overheard some riveting conversations. We have also made lovely, lasting friendships.

This service really comes into its own in high season when the roads are badly crowded. Then it really is a case of letting the train take the strain. But do book early.

Rail, generally, is a good way to get around France, particularly as French Railways offer an amazing selection of deals. There are family tickets, rover tickets, student tickets, *troisième age* (third age) tickets, which also apply to British senior citizens on the production of a special card that you can buy at most main-line stations in Britain. This is quite separate from the normal British travel card for the elderly, and costs around £7, but the saving on tickets can be as much as 50% – though this does not apply to the price of putting a car on the train or *wagon-lits*.

Some of these services can be booked through British Rail. Speak to your travel agent and, if you are travelling with small children, keep in mind that some long-distance French trains even have a nursery aboard.

On one occasion when we needed to come back to England for a brief period in the middle of our summer stay in France, we decided against flying and travelled by the TGV, spending a night in Paris before carrying on to Calais-Dover-London the next day. The TGV (*Train Grande Vitesse*) is the French high-speed train, which looks a bit like a bullet and gets from Paris to Nice in about seven hours. Between Nice and Marseilles the speeds are generally less spectacular; the TGV needs a straight track and it cannot whizz through the mountains and along the twisting coast road at high speeds as it can on its own special tracks. The fastest part of the journey is between Lyon and Paris. This will change. The French are planning a new Paris-Nice track that will take a different route. The *vignerons* of the area where the route will run are protesting about the damage this will cause to their vineyards, but they are unlikely to win in the end. The French government usually do what they plan, and since they are much more generous with compensation than our own government, perhaps the battle will not be too bloody.

We enjoyed our trip on the TGV. You must book in advance, and your seat is then reserved. Your ticket tells you your seat number and the number of the compartment in which you will travel. At all the stations where the TGV stops, the compartment numbers are marked on the platform, so you can wait in the exact place. Inside, the seating is arranged like that on an aircraft and is extremely comfortable. It looks as if there is little leg-room on arrival in the carriage, but in fact the seating is not cramped for normal-sized people. There are excellent buffet cars scattered along the train (try the *croque-monsieur* it's great) and those who travel first-class can eat in a comfortable restaurant. The fascinating thing about the train is its smoothness and silence. I found I could use my small desk-top computer without the slightest difficulty as there is so little rocking, rolling and bumping. The train glides through spectacular scenery and through parts of France that are some distance from roads. If you want to get the feel of the country you can do just that on the TGV.

With both Germany and Italy developing equally fast train systems, the turn of the century could herald the return of rail travel as *the* way to see Europe. Never having liked aeroplanes, I can't wait.

9

A Maison of your Own

It has recently become not only popular but simpler to buy your own property in France. A home of your own in France, depending on the location, can be remarkably cheap, though the sudden influx of British has increased the price of property. Do remember, though, that the further South you get in your search for a property, the more expensive that property becomes. The North of France offers bargains at anything from £30,000 upwards – less for something tumble-down – but the weather is going to be much the same as we suffer anywhere in Britain and your heating bills heavier. Electricity in France is extremely expensive.

The other thing to take into account is getting there. France is a very big country. If you want what is called a *maison secondaire* and choose the less expensive areas, like the Drôme, or the Ardèche, where the weather is beautiful in the summer, you'll be hard put to pop down for the weekend and travel can become an added expense. If it is a holiday home you want, settle upon somewhere either in reasonable driving distance from Britain, or where there is a main-line rail service or an airport. Remember, though, that these amenities automatically put up the price of property, just as they would in Britain.

If this is to be your permanent home, it perhaps doesn't matter that you have chosen somewhere inaccessible – except for the chore of picking up your guests, who will be

arriving at some airport miles away. When you have a
home in France, believe me, you have lots of guests –
usually uninvited and always in the summer.

If your dream home is set in the Côte d'Azur, you will
be talking about mega-money for the villa with pool and
palm-trees that everyone covets. But it is possible to buy
in the South without bankrupting yourself. Village houses,
particularly in the Var, the area to the West of the
Alpes-Maritimes which begins the other side of Cannes
and Grasse, go for around £85,000. Village houses are tall
and thin, usually with a *cave* and three floors, with two
rooms on each floor. The advantage: if you are prepared to
learn French and make friends, you are immediately part
of French village life. The disadvantage: there is rarely a
garden or anywhere to sit out and this can become frus-
trating on a wonderfully sunny day. And since most days
are wonderfully sunny in summer, unless you dislike sun-
bathing, that can add up to a lot of frustration.

If, however, it is the Riviera life that appeals, prices are
much lower in the Var than on the coast or in the hills
behind the Côte d'Azur. The terrain is different – wilder
and less sophisticated and, when you have woven your
way down the mountains to the coast, the beaches are not
manicured. But life there is cheaper. There is a lot of
modern building which is reasonably priced, usually in
apartment projects centered around a swimming pool, but
this sort of property can be seen everywhere else in the
world, and may not be what you seek. It is the old, interesting houses that cost the most and that are the most
desirable.

If you have made up your mind to buy, do make sure
you see the area in all seasons before you take the plunge.
What is delightful in summer can be cold, miserable and
cut off in the depth of winter. As much as we love Les
Eygages, we really would not want to spend the entire
winter there. It gets cold. And lonely.

As in Britain, it is best to start with an estate agent,
though in France there are other methods. Our dry-
cleaning lady in Grasse was advertising what sounded like
a delightful apartment for sale in the centre of the old
town from a handwritten notice pinned up on her till. The
local supermarkets carry the same kind of notice and in
our area there is a give-away sheet, called *06*, which prints

a great many adverts for inexpensive property. So it is best to immerse yourself in the area you fancy before making a final choice.

You will need a *notaire* to do the deal for you – you'll find them listed in the Yellow Pages, but if possible it is best to go by recommendation. *Notaires* also often have knowledge of property that never officially comes up for sale. French law, in which no child of the family can be disinherited, can cause a lot of complications when it comes to selling property, as each child has an equal share and say in the matter.

There is also a system called *achat en viager*, a life annuity purchase used when the seller is elderly and has no heirs. The *notaire* works out the value of the house; you pay a lump sum, usually around a third, and then a monthly index-linked annuity worked out according to the age of the seller. Payments stop at his or her death and the property is yours. This is all very well if the seller has a normal life span; not so good if they live to be over 100. And it is an unattractive proposition to be waiting for someone to die.

The legalities of buying a home in France are completely different from those in England and Wales. You can't be 'gazumped', but there is an awful lot of small print that you must get translated so that you understand exactly what you are letting yourself in for.

Having chosen your house, you put down a deposit of 10% on the price agreed (which cannot now be changed) and sign a *Promesse de Vente* or a *Compromis*. Both are promises between you and the vendor to buy and sell the house, but there is a slight difference between the two. The *Promesse de Vente* allows you to think things over, but even so, you lose your deposit if you change your mind. A *Compromis* commits you to buy. There is no going back, unless you can produce documentary evidence that you cannot raise the money and your applications for a loan have been turned down. Do make sure that this particular get-out clause is written into your contract before you sign.

After this comes the *Acte de Vente*, which we would call the Deed of Sale. At this stage you pay the rest of the money and the property is transferred to you.

If there is difficulty in raising the money, you can buy

property in France on an instalment basis, putting down about 5% of the price and paying rent on a promise to settle the rest of the purchase price, usually in two or three years' time. If you still cannot raise the money, you lose your downpayment and your rent.

It is possible to borrow money in France, and usually the interest rates are lower than in Britain, but if it is a mortgage you are after, it could prove easier to obtain one in Britain. Both Barclays Bank and the National Westminster Bank have mortgage schemes for foreign property and can also supply you with useful printed information.

Make sure you do everything legally. The vendor may suggest to you that you pay some of the price 'under the table' – in other words, in cash between the two of you, so that you will pay smaller fees to the *notaire*. The real reason is that this is a tax dodge for the vendor. Should you ever sell your house for the price that you really paid, you will find that you are liable for the French version of capital gains tax on what looks like profit but isn't. The only winner in this case is the vendor.

Living in France can be wonderful. The quality of life, with its emphasis on food and comfort, is quite different from that in Britain. We spend money on decorating our homes; the French spend it on taking the entire family out to lunch every Sunday. Priorities are different. But remember that you are a guest, and that the French, particularly in big cities and small towns, may be wary of you. It is a real honour to be invited into a Frenchman's home. His maison is *his* château and he is choosy about who comes through the front door.

You could be cut off living full-time in France. Areas such as the Côte d'Azur, the Dordogne and, increasingly, the Var have a lot of English-speaking residents. But if you want to make the most of your time in France, and became a real part of the community, please, please take French lessons. They can open up a whole new way of life.

10

Hotel and Restaurant Directory

PLEASE NOTE: When dialling in France, use all eight and, in the case of Paris and surroundings, nine figures. When dialling from Britain dial 010 33 followed by the number.

ABRICOTINE

Route de Romans, 26200 Tain l'Hermitage, Drôme (Télé: 75.07.44.60)

Closed 20 Nov–4 Dec and Sun from Nov–March.

ALOUETTES, Les

4 Rue Antonin Barye, 77630 Barbizon, Seine-et-Marne (Télé: 1.60.66.41.98)

Open all year.

AMBASSADEUR

Buffet Gare, Place Foch, 62000 Arras, Pas-de-Calais (Télé: 21.23.29.80)

Open all year.

ANGLETERRE, Hôtel d'

19 Place Mgr Tissier, 51000 Châlons-sur-Marne, Marne (Télé: 26.68.21.51)

Closed 21 July–12 Aug, Christmas, Sat midday and Sun except bank holidays.

AUBERGE DE LA PLAINE

La Rothière, 10500 Brienne-le-Château, Aube
(Télé: 25.92.21.79)

Closed 21 Dec–5 Jan and Fri evenings.

AUBERGE DES QUATRE SAISONS

26130 St Restitut, Drôme
(Télé: 75.04.71.88)

Closed 2–30 Jan; restaurant closed Sat lunchtime.

AUBERGE DES ROSIERS

8 Quai Mallarmé, 77870 Vulaines-sur-Seine,
Seine-et-Marne
(Télé: 1.64.23.71.61 & 1.64.23.92.38)

Closed last week of Aug and 1–4 Sept; Feb school holidays (variable dates).

AUBERGE LA GRANGE AUX LOUPS

8 Rue du 11 Novembre, 60300 Apremont, Oise
(Télé: 44.25.33.79)

Closed 15 days in Dec; Sun evenings and all Mon.

AUBERGE ST VINCENT

Rue St Vincent, 51150 Ambonnay, Marne
(Télé: 26.57.01.98)

Restaurant closed Sun night and all Mon.

BAS-BREAU

22 Rue Grande, 77630 Barbizon, Seine-et-Marne
(Télé: 1.60.66.40.05)

Closed 2 Jan–2 Feb.

BEAU RIVAGE, *Hôtel*

2 Rue Beau-Rivage, 69420 Condrieu, Rhône
(Télé: 74.59.52.24)

Open all year.

BEC FIN, *Restaurant*

7 Place Saint-Maurice, 38200 Vienne, Isère
(Télé: 74.85.76.72)

Closed Sun evenings, Mon.

BEFFROI, *Le*

4 Grande Rue, 21700 Nuits-St-Georges, Côte-d'Or
(Télé: 80.61.01.27)

BELLE ETOILE, *Hôtel-restaurant*

Z.A. Les Alouettes, 62223 St-Nicolas-les-Arras,
Pas-de-Calais
(Télé: 21.58.59.00)

Restaurant closed Sun evenings and bank holiday
evenings.

BELLEVUE

416 Quai Lamartine, 71000 Mâcon, Saône-et-Loire
(Télé: 85.38.05.07)

Open all year.

BELLEVUE, *Hôtel-restaurant*

38370 Les Roches-de-Condrieu, Isère
(Télé: 74.56.41.42)

Closed 4–13 Oct, 15 Feb–11 Mar, Sun nights from Oct
to Mar, Tues lunch from April to Sep and all Mon.

BRASSERIE DU RHÔNE

56 Place Carnot, 69400 Villefranche-sur-Saône, Rhône
(Télé: 74.65.28.85)

Open all year.

CAFE BOURGUIGNON

La Place d'Armes, 71150 Chagny, Saône-et-Loire
(Télé: 85.87.17.98)

Open all year.

CAPITELLE, La

26270 Mirmande, Drôme
(Télé: 75.63.02.72)

Restaurant closed 15 Nov–15 Jan, Wed midday and Tues.

CHANZY

8 Rue Chanzy, 62000 Arras, Pas-de-Calais
(Télé: 21.71.02.02)

Open all year.

CHAPEAU ROUGE

5 Rue Michelet, 21000 Dijon, Côte-d'Or
(Télé: 80.30.28.10)

Open all year.

CHAUMIERE, *Hostellerie de la*

10200 Arsonval, Aube
(Télé: 25.27.91.02)

Closed Sun evenings and all Mon, except bank holidays.

CHEVAL BLANC, Le

Rue du Moulin, 51400 Sept-Saulx, Marne
(Télé: 26.03.90.27)

Closed mid Jan-mid Feb.

CLOCHE, *Hôtel de la*

14 Place Darcy, 21000 Dijon, Côte-d'Or
(Télé: 80.30.12.32)

Open all year.

COMMERCE, *Hôtel du*

28 Rue Gambetta, 62000 Arras, Pas-de-Calais
(Télé: 21.71.10.07)

Open all year.

COMMERCE, *Hôtel du*

Rue République, 10110 Bar-sur-Seine, Aube
(Télé: 25.29.86.36)

Closed 25 Sept–16 Oct.

COMMERCE, *Hôtel-restaurant du*

71150 Rully, Saône-et-Loire
(Télé: 85.87.20.09)

Closed 15 Dec–end of Jan and Wednesdays.

COTE D'OR

2 Rue Argentine, 21210 Saulieu, Côte-d'Or
(Télé: 80.64.07.66)

Open all year.

COTE ST JACQUES, *La*

14 Faubourg de Paris, 89300 Joigny, Yonne
(Télé: 86.62.09.70)

Closed from 2 Jan–31 Jan.

DEUX COTEAUX, *Hôtel*

18 Rue Joseph Péala, 26600 Tain l'Hermitage, Drôme
(Télé: 75.08.33.01)

Closed 15–29 Feb, Fri and Sat from Oct to Jan.

FAIDHERBE, *Hôtel*

12 Rue Faidherbe, 62200 Boulogne-sur-Mer,
Pas-de-Calais
(Télé: 21.31.60.93)

Open all year.

FAISANDERIE, *La*

45 Grand-Place, 62000 Arras, Pas-de-Calais
(Télé: 21.48.20.76)

Closed 5–19 Aug and 23–30 Dec and Feb, Sun evenings
and all Mon.

FIN-DE-SIECLE, Restaurant
46 Place du Clos, 84300 Cavaillon, Vaucluse
(Télé: 90.71.12.27)
Closed 25 Aug–20 Sept and Wed.

FLANDRE, Le Bistrot de
2 Rue d'Amiens, 60200 Compiègne, Oise
(Télé: 44.83.26.35)
Open all year.

FLORENCE, Le
43 Boulevard Foch, 51100 Reims, Marne
(Télé: 26.47.12.70)
Closed 30 July–17 Oct.

FONTAINE BLEUE, La
18 Rue J. Moulin, 69400 Villefranche-sur-Saône, Rhône
(Télé: 74.68.10.37)
Closed 21 Dec–15 Jan, Sat lunchtime from Sept–June,
Sun lunchtime in July and August.

FORET-D'OTHE, Café-restaurant de la
10160 Maraye-en-Othe, Aube
(Télé: 25.70.11.08)
Open all year.

FRANCE ET ANGLETERRE, Hôtel
28 Rue Emile Zola, 02100 St Quentin, Aisne
(Télé: 23.62.13.10)
Open all year.

GABETIERE, La
38780 Estrablin, Vienne
(Télé: 74.58.01.31)
Open all year.

GARBURE
3 Rue Joseph Ducos, 84230 Châteauneuf-du-Pape, Vaucluse
(Télé: 90.83.75.08)
Closed August.

GENTILHOMMIERE, La
13 Vallée de la Serrée, 21700 Nuits-St-Georges, Côte-d'Or
(Télé: 80.61.12.06)
Closed end of Dec to end of Jan; restaurant closed Tues lunchtime and all Mon except bank holidays.

GIFFON, *Hôtel-restaurant*
Place de l'Eglise, 26400 Grane, Drôme
(Télé: 75.62.60.64)
Closed Feb, Sun evening from 1 Oct to 1 May and Mon, except bank holidays.

GRAND HOTEL CLEMENT
91 Esplanade du Mal-Leclerc, 62610 Ardres, Pas-de-Calais
(Télé: 21.82.25.25)
Closed 15 Jan–15 Feb, all Mon and Tues lunchtime from mid Oct-March.

GRAND HOTEL ET RESTAURANT LE PRESIDENT
6 Rue Dachery, 02100 St Quentin, Aisne
(Télé: 23.62.69.77)
Open all year. Restaurant closed 29 July–26 Aug, 23 Dec–2 Jan, Sun evenings and all Mon.

GRAND HOTEL NEGRE COSTE
33 Cours Mirabeau, 13100 Aix-en-Provence, Bouches-du-Rhône
(Télé: 42.27.74.22)
Open all year.

GRAND ST JEAN, Hôtel au
18 Rue du Faubourg Madeleine, 21200 Beaune
(Télé: 80.24.12.22)
Closed 20 Nov–15 Jan.

GREUZE, Restaurant
1 Rue A. Thibaudet, 71700 Tournus, Saône-et-Loire
(Télé: 85.51.13.52)
Closed 1–10 Dec.

GREUZE, Hôtel de
5 Rue A. Thibaudet, 71700 Tournus, Saône-et-Loire
(Télé: 85.40.77.77)
Open all year.

HALLE, Hôtel-restaurant de la
Place Halle, 71640 Givry, Saône-et-Loire
(Télé: 85.44.32.45)
Closed Nov, Sun evenings and all Mon.

HALTE OK
Echangeur A7, 38150 Chanas, Isère
(Télé: 74.84.27.50)
Hotel open all year; restaurant closed midday Sat and all Sun.

HARLAY
3 Rue Harlay, 60200 Compiègne, Oise
(Télé: 44.23.01.50)
Closed 14 Dec–6 Jan.

HOLIDAY INN GARDEN COURT
Bd Alliés, 62100 Calais, Pas-de-Calais
(Télé: 21.34.69.69)
Open all year.

IBIS

Rue Greuze, 62100 Calais, Pas-de-Calais
(Télé: 21.96.69.69)

Open all year.

IBIS

Route Nationale 30080, 60300 Senlis, Oise
(Télé: 44.53.70.50)

Open all year.

JOUBERT, *Hôtel*

9 Place Général Joubert, 01190 Pont-de-Vaux, Ain
(Télé: 85.30.30.55)

Closed 5–20 Jan.

LAMELOISE

36 Place d'Armes, 71150 Chagny, Saône-et-Loire
(Télé: 85.87.08.85)

Closed 19 Dec–17 Jan. Restaurant closed all Wed and Thurs lunchtime.

LIEGEOISE, *La*

10 Rue A. Monsigny, 62200 Boulogne-sur-Mer, Pas-de-Calais
(Télé: 21.31.61.15)

Closed 15–31 July, Sun evenings and all Wed.

LONGO MAI

Le Sambuc, 13200 Arles, Bouches-du-Rhône
(Télé: 90.97.21.91)

Closed Feb; restaurant closed midday, except Sun.

MAGDELEINE

31 Av. P. Sémard, 26100 Romans, Drôme
(Télé: 75.02.33.53)

Closed Sun except July and Aug.

MARRONNIERS D'ARC, *Les*

16 Rue de Dijon, 21560 Arc-sur-Tille, Côte-d'Or
(Télé: 80.37.09.62)

Closed Mon.

MAZARIN

13 Cours Mirabeau, 13100 Aix-en-Provence
(Télé: 42.27.62.86)

Open all year.

MERCURE

Centre Commercial, 38670 Chasse-sur-Rhône, Isère
(Télé: 72.24.29.29)

Open all year.

MERCURE (*Mâcon*)

Aire de St Albain, Autoroute A6, 71260 St Albain,
Saône-et-Loire
(Télé: 85.33.19.00)

Open all year.

MINISTERE, *Hôtel du*

31 Rue Surène, 75008 Paris
(Télé: 1.42.66.21.43)

Open all year.

MIRVY

Route de Manosque, 84240 La Bastide-des-Jourdans,
Vaucluse
(Télé: 90.77.83.23)

Closed 3–9 Oct; restaurant closed Wed midday in season, Tues evening and all Wed outside season.

NOVOTEL

Echangeur Mâcon, Route A6, Mâcon Nord,
Saône-et-Loire
(Télé: 85.36.00.80)

Open all year.

PAIX, Hôtel de la

9 Rue Buirette, 51100 Reims, Marne
(Télé: 26.40.04.08)

Open all year.

PARC, Hôtel du

Place du Clos, 84300 Cavaillon
(Télé: 90.71.57.78)

Open all year.

PARIS ET POSTE, Hôtel

97 Rue République, 89100 Sens, Yonne
(Télé: 86.65.17.43)

Open all year.

PARIS-NICE, Hôtel

43 Rue de Marseille, 38150 Chanas, Isère
(Télé: 74.84.21.22)

Open all year.

PARIS-NICE, Hôtel-restaurant

Rondpont de la Résistance, 89300 Joigny, Yonne
(Télé: 86.62.06.72)

Closed Sun evenings and all Mon.

PERRON, Hôtel du

9 Rue Général Leclerc, 45240 La Ferté-St-Aubin,
Loiret
(Télé: 38.76.53.36)

Closed 4–18 Feb, Sun evening and Mon 1 Dec–15 Mar.

PETITE AUBERGE

105 Av. A Renoir, 06520 Magagnosc, Alpes-Maritimes
(Télé: 93.42.75.32)

Closed July, Feb school holidays (variable dates), Tues
evening in Winter (except hotel) and all Wed.

PLAISANCE, Hôtel

96 Av. Libération, 69400 Villefranche-sur-Saône,
Rhône
(Télé: 74.65.33.52)

Closed 24 Dec–1 Jan.

POELON, Le

13 Route Nationale, 21560 Arc-sur-Tille, Côte-d'Or
(Télé: 80.37.21.52)

Closed Sat evening and all Sun.

PONTON, Restaurant

40 Place Jacquemart, 26100 Romans, Drôme
(Télé: 75.02.29.91)

Closed 15–31 July, 4–11 Feb, Sun evenings, Tues.

POSTE

1 Rue Grillot, 21210 Saulieu, Côte-d'Or
(Télé: 80.64.05.67)

Open all year.

POSTE, Hostellerie de la

13 Place Vauban, 89200 Avallon, Yonne
(Télé: 86.34.06.12)

Hotel open all year. Restaurant closed Mon and Tues
lunchtime.

POSTE, Hôtel de la

Place de la Libération, 21320 Pouilly-en-Auxois,
Côte-d'Or
(Télé: 80.90.86.44)

Closed 24 Nov–9 Dec.

RECRE, La

8 Place du Taurobole, 26600 Tain l'Hermitage, Drôme
(Télé: 75.08.19.00)

Closed 1–15 Oct.

RELAIS DE L'EMPEREUR
1 Place M. Dormoy, 26200 Montélimar, Drôme
(Télé: 75.01.29.00)
Closed 11 Nov–22 Dec.

RELAIS DES GOUVERNEURS
38 Rue Nationale, 10200 Bar-sur-Aube, Aube
(Télé: 25.27.08.76)
Closed 15–24 Feb.

RELAIS DU MACONNAIS
La Croix Blanche, 71960 Pierreclos, Saône-et-Loire
(Télé: 85.36.60.72)
Closed 3 Jan–3 Feb, Sun evenings and Mon out of
season.

RELAIS FLEURI
Route Saulieu, 89200 Avallon, Yonne
(Télé: 86.34.02.85)
Open all year.

RICHE, Le
10 Rue des Toiles, 02100 St Quentin, Aisne
(Télé: 23.62.33.53)
Closed 8 July–6 Aug, Sun evenings and all Tues.

ROYAL CHAMPAGNE
Bellevue, 51160 Champillon, Marne
(Télé: 26.52.87.11)
Open all year.

SAUVAGE, Le
Place Champ de Mars, 71700 Tournus, Saône-et-Loire
(Télé: 85.51.14.45)
Closed 11 Nov–19 Dec.

ST-GEORGES, *Le*

32 Avenue Jean-Jaurès, 71100 Chalon-sur-Saône,
Saône-et-Loire
(Télé: 85.48.27.05)

Hotel open all year; restaurant closed Sat midday.

ST JEAN, *Hôtel*

24 Quai Gambetta, 71100 Chalon-sur-Saône,
Saône-et-Loire
(Télé: 85.48.45.65)

Open all year.

ST-MAURICE, *Restaurant*

Place Saint-Maurice, 38200 Vienne, Isère
(Télé: 74.85.08.48)

Closed 1 May and 25 Dec.

SULLY, *Le*

97 Quai Henri-IV, 76200 Dieppe, Seine-Maritime
(Télé: 35.84.23.13)

Closed 15 Nov–15 Dec, Tues evenings, all Wed.

TERMINUS

21 Av. Gambetta, 71700 Tournus, Saône-et-Loire
(Télé: 85.51.05.54)

Closed 14–21 Nov, 3–24 Jan, Tues evenings and Wed
except July and August.

UNIVERS

3 Place Croix-Rouge, 62000 Arras, Pas-de-Calais
(Télé: 21.71.34.01)

Open all year.

11

Complicated Routes

Reaching the A26 autoroute from the port of Dunkerque

From Dunkerque take the **N225** out of town, direction Lille, for 13km until it joins the **A25** autoroute.

Follow the **A25** to Steenvoorde.

Leave the **A25** at Steenvoorde (Exit 13) and follow the signs for Hazebrouck (**D37** then **D916**, 15km).

At Hazebrouck follow direction Béthune (**D916** then **D937**, 26km).

At Béthune follow **N41**, signposted Arras and **A26** autoroute.

You will find the entrance to the **A26** 3km from the centre of Béthune.

Country route: Calais-Chartres-Autoroute du Sud

Take **A26** autoroute out of Calais. Leave autoroute at exit 4, Thérouanne and take **D157** which becomes **D126** signposted Hesdin.

After the village of Wandonne, about 12km after leaving autoroute, turn left on to **D928**, again signposted Hesdin (24km).

From here take Abbeville direction, **D928** all the way (85km).

At Abbeville take **N28** to Rouen (100km).

At Rouen follow Paris **A13** autoroute signs which take you round the East of Rouen.

⋆ Remain on autoroute **A13** for 12km, coming off at exit 19, Louviers – Evreux signs.

Take **N154** to Evreux (52km). At Evreux take ring road round town looking for Nonancourt and Dreux signposts. This remains the **N154**.

At Nonancourt (42km) turn left on the **N12** – this road by-passes Nonancourt – for Dreux.

In 16km, after by-passing Dreux by remaining on **N12**, swing right on to ring road signposted Chartres and in 4km rejoin the **N154** to Chartres (32km).

To join **A6** autoroute South from Chartres, using the autoroutes, take **A11** autoroute (which becomes **A10** near Ponthévrard) to Paris for about 80km until motorways merge and become the **A6** at Chilly-Mazarin.

Be sure to take **A6** (Autoroute du Soleil) Fontainebleau – Lyon signs at this point: not Paris.

The better and shorter alternative is to take the **A11** from Chartres, leaving after 23km at the Etampes exit and by-passing Ablis.

Take the **N191** to Etampes (30km) and thence through Etampes to the **D837**, signposted Milly-la-Forêt (25km) and Fontainebleau.

Milly-la-Forêt has a bypass, but do not use it. Go into the town (follow *centre ville* signs). You are looking for the **D16**, signposted Nemours.

Stay on the **D16** for 12km until you reach the little town of La Chapelle-la-Reine. Turn left out of the town on to the **N152** which in 3km leads on to the Autoroute du Soleil.

Caen-Paris country route

From docks follow Paris signs.

In Caen take Paris direction via **N13** signs.

Continue on **N13** through Lisieux (44km) then Evreux (72km).

Continue on **N13** through Evreux following Paris signs.

In 27km, 9km after the village of Pacy, you will join the Autoroute de Normandie (**A13**) for the Paris Périphérique.

⋆ Travellers from Caen, Le Havre or Dieppe who wish to see Chartres can pick up the route from here.

Dieppe-Paris

Take the **N27** out of Dieppe, direction Rouen. Stay on this road for 42km.

Just after the village of Fresquienne, to the right you will see autoroute signs for Rouen.

This leads to autoroute **A15** and the ring road (**N15**) round Rouen.

Stay on the **N15** until it connects with the **A13** autoroute de Normandie for Paris and the Périphérique.

To the Auberge des Rosiers, Vulaines-sur-Seine from the A6

Vulaines is much simpler to get to if you are going South.

Come off the autoroute (**A6**) at the Melun exit and on to the **N7**. In 11km you come to Pringy.

Here, the **N7** veers off right; you go straight on, taking the **N472**.

Do not go into Melun. You will come to a big roundabout.

Take the **D142** to Fontainebleau and, in 5km, take the **D138**, which will lead you straight through the Fontainebleau woods and to Vulaines-sur-Seine.

If you are driving North, come off the **A6** autoroute at the Sens exit.

Take the Sens road (**N60**) briefly until on your left appears the **D103** to Cheroy.

At Cheroy take the **D225**, signposted Nemours.

After 8km turn right to Lorrez-le-Bocage (2km) and in Lorrez, look for the signposts to Moret on the **D218** on the left. You'll know you are nearly at Moret when 18km later, you cross the **N6** on to the **D39**. This road ambles alongside the river for about 8km until it runs into the **D210** where you must turn left and in no time at all (3km) you will find yourself at the bridge at Vulaines with the hotel on the right.

The Country Run from Bierre to Arras

Leave the **A6** autoroute at Bierre-les-Semur and take the **D980** to Montbard, by-passing Semur-en-Auxois (about 26km).

At Montbard take the **D905** (on the left just after the

railway and *before* the town bridge) to Ancy-le-Franc and Tonnerre (44km).

At Tonnerre continue on the **D905** for 10km and then turn right just before the village of Charrey on to the **D374** for Marolles s/s Lignières – Ervy-le-Chatel – Auxon (23km). At Auxon turn left briefly on to the **N77** where the **D374** continues almost immediately on the right.

In 9km along the **D374** you come to Maraye-en-Othe.

Leaving Maraye-en-Othe continue for 16.5km to Paisy Cosdon. Continue along the **D374** crossing the **N60** and on to Marcilly-le-Hayer (15km).

From Marcilly take the **D54** in the direction of Nogent-sur-Seine. Ten kilometres out of Marcilly you come to Avant-lès-Marcilly. Here turn right on to the **D52** for Ferreux (5km).

Continue along the **D52** to Pont-sur-Seine crossing the **N19** (8km).

Take the **D52** through Barbuise to Villenauxe-la-Grande, where you pick up the **D248** which joins the **D48** to Esternay (28km).

Go through Esternay taking the **D48** Montmirail road through Champguyon and Morsaine where it becomes the **D375**.

If at this point you want to speed up you can take the Meaux road and then to Senlis and the autoroute.

Continuing cross-country, in Montmirail take the **D41** to Artonges (7km) then the **D20** to Condé-en-Brie (9km).

At Condé-en-Brie turn left on to the **D4** and through St Eugène–Crezancy–Mézy–Epieds (16km).

At Epieds take the **D967** to Fère-en-Tardenois (13km).

At Fère-en-Tardenois take the **D6** in the direction of Soissons. After about 10km turn right on to the **D22** for Braine (11km).

At Braine take the **D14** to Vailly-sur-Aisne (9km).

Take the **D15**, in the direction of Laon, for 11km where the road joins the **N2** as you near Urcel.

Here, turn left to stay on the **N2** and head for Chavignon, 3km away.

At Chavignon take the **D19** to Pinon (5km).

At Pinon take the Coucy-le-Château-Auffrique road (**D14**, then **D5**, 13km).

At Coucy, take the St Quentin road to the **D1** (2km).

At St Quentin, pick up the Calais autoroute (**A26**).

The Western Route from Chartres to Vienne

Leave Chartres on the **N154**, direction Orléans.

In 53km you will reach Artenay and the entrance to the **A10** autoroute.

Remain on this autoroute until you bear off on to the **A71** autoroute which runs in a southerly direction past Orléans, Bourges, Clermont-Ferrand (313km).

At Clermont-Ferrand join the **A72** autoroute, direction St Etienne (146km).

Above St Etienne, join **A47**, direction Vienne, joining **A7** just after Givors (34km), direction Vienne – Marseilles.

To La Gabetière, Estrablin, from the A7 Autoroute at Vienne

Leave autoroute at Vienne and follow *centre ville* signs until you see signposts to Pont-Evêque.

In 3km you reach Pont-Evêque. Go into town centre and out other side on **D502**. Estrablin is approximately 6km and to the left off the road. You will see signposts to the Gabetière on the left.

From Tain l'Hermitage to Montélimar South, via Crest

Leaving **A7** at Tain, take Romans road (**D532**, 15km).

At Romans, briefly take Valence road (**N532**). After Bourg-de-Péage take left fork on to **D538**, signposted Crest.

For Giffon Hotel at Grane, cross River Drôme in Crest, then turn right on to **D104**, signposted Loriol. Grane is 8km away.

To continue from Crest to Montélimar, take **D538** from Crest to La Répara (7km).

At La Répara take **D6** to Cléon-d'Andran (11km).

At Cléon, take **D9** through to Grignan (28km).

At Grignan take **D541** signposted Montélimar (18km). You will cross the autoroute and at this point will see the signs directing you back on to it.

From Cavaillon to La Bastide-des-Jourdans and Aix-en-Provence

Leave autoroute **A7** at Cavaillon exit, direction Pertuis (**D973**, 45km).

Just before Pertuis take the left turn on to the **D119**.

This runs into the **D956**; 17km along this road is La Bastide-des-Jourdans.

To reach Aix-en-Provence, return to Pertuis and follow Aix signposts. In 3.5km you will be directed on to the autoroute that takes you round Aix and back on the Autoroute du Soleil.

Bonne route!

12
Road Signs

ABSENCE DE GLISSIERE
no crash barrier

ABSENCE DE MARQUAGE
no lines drawn in the road

ACCOTEMENT NON STABILISEE
soft verge

ARROSAGE AUTOMATIQUE
the road may be being automatically watered; shut your windows

ATTENTION TRAVAUX
road works ahead

AUTRES DIRECTIONS
if your destination is not signposted, follow this sign until it is

AVEC PIECES DE MONNAIE
the channel to use at a *péage* if you have the right change

BETTERAVES
beetroots on road from harvesting

BOUE
mud on road

BROUILLARD
a stretch of road inclined to fog

CENTRE VILLE
to the town centre

CHAUSSEE DEFORMEE
uneven road surface

COTE DE STATIONNEMENT
the side of the road on which parking is permitted

DEGAGEMENT A DROITE AUTHORISE APRES UN TEMPS D'ARRET
by a traffic light: you can filter to the right even if the light is still red providing you have stopped and it is safe to do so

ECHANGEUR
motorway exits and entrances, where they divide

ESSAYEZ VOTRE FREINS
try your brakes

ETEINDREZ VOS FEUX
turn out your lights

FREINS
brakes

GLISSIERE
a barrier, usually in the centre of the autoroute

GRAVILLONS
gravel on the road

*LA BANDE D'ARRET D'URGENCE EST
RESERVEE AUX VEHICLES DE SECOURS*

the hard shoulder can only be driven on by break-down
vehicles

ORNIERAGE

ruts

PARKING GRATUIT

free parking

PARKING GENANT

if you park here you are making a nuisance of yourself
and will be towed away

PASSAGE INTERDIT

you aren't allowed there

PEAGE

where you take a ticket to get on an autoroute or pay to
come off

PIQUE-NIQUE JEUX D'ENFANTS

a stopping place for picnics and where there are also
children's games

PNEUS SOUS GONFLEES – DANGER followed by
STATION DE GONFLAGE GRATUIT

a warning that soft tyres are dangerous and telling you
that in a short distance there will be a place where you
can check the tyre pressures without charge

POIDS LOURDS

heavy vehicles

PRENEZ UN TICKET

take a ticket from the machine, either at an autoroute
péage or at a parking area

PRIORITE AUX PIETONS

give way to pedestrians

PROCHAINE SERVICE STATION
next filling station

PROCHAINE SORTIE
next exit

PRODUIT REGIONAUX
a shop, usually on an autoroute, where they sell products of the area

PRUDENCE
take care, be prudent

RACCORDEMENT PROVISIONAIRE
a temporary junction ahead

RALENTIR
slow down

RAPPEL
simply means 'remember', usually warning you about speeding

REFUGE
you are coming to a place where you can pull in off the road; usually on an autoroute

RESPECTEZ LA SIGNALISATION
follow whatever signals are being given

RISQUE D'ATTENTE
you may be held up by traffic

RISQUE D'INONDATION
risk of flooding

ROULEZ DOUCEMENT
drive slowly

ROULEZ A PAS
drive at walking speed

ROUTE BARREE
the road is blocked or barred

SIGNAL AUTOMATIQUE
usually on a level crossing, meaning that a barrier will come down automatically if a train is coming

SORTIE DE CAMIONS
lorry exit

SORTIE D'USINE
factory exit

TIRS DE MINES
you are near a mine and there will be blasting – don't jump out of your skin

TOUAGE
towing

TOUTES DIRECTIONS
(all directions): signposts in towns leading you towards signposts to other destinations

TRAVAUX
is nothing to do with travelling; it means road works

TRAVAUX D'ELARGISSEMENT
they are widening the road

TRAVERSEE INTERDIT POUR LOURDS
no through road for drivers of heavy lorries

TROP VITE, TROP PRES . . . DANGER
driving too fast and too close to the car in front is dangerous

UN TRAIN PEUT CACHER UN AUTRE

only seen on level crossings, warning that one train can hide another, so make sure the line really is clear

UTILISEZ VOTRE FREIN MOTEUR RETROGRADEUR

(usually on a steep hill): get into a lower gear and use your engine to brake

VEHICULES LENTŜ VOIE A DROITE

(usually on a steep hill): slow vehicles (such as lorries) must use the right hand lane; so must you, if you are driving an old banger

VERGLAS

black ice

VERGLAS FREQUENT

black ice often on the road

VERIFIEZ VOTRE DISTANCE DE SECURITE followed by *1 MARQUE . . . DANGER*; *2 MARQUES . . . SECURITE*

arrows on the autoroute, asking you to leave two arrows between you and the car in front.

VIRAGE DANGEREUX

dangerous bend

VIRAGES POUR 2 KILOMETRES

the road bends for two (or whatever) kilometres

VOIE RETRECIE

road narrows, where two lanes become one, for instance

ZONE DE TRAVAUX

an area of roadworks ahead

13

Identifying Number Plates

01	Ain	26	Drôme
02	Aisne	27	Eure
03	Allier	28	Eure-et-Loir
04	Alpes-de-Haute-Provence	29	Finistère
05	Alpes (Hautes)	30	Gard
06	Alpes-Maritimes	31	Garonne (Haute)
07	Ardèche	32	Gers
08	Ardennes	33	Gironde
09	Ariège	34	Hérault
10	Aube	35	Ille-et-Vilaine
11	Aude	36	Indre
12	Aveyron	37	Indre-et-Loire
13	Bouches-du-Rhône	38	Isère
14	Calvados	39	Jura
15	Cantal	40	Landes
16	Charente	41	Loir-et-Cher
17	Charente-Maritime	42	Loire
18	Cher	43	Loire (Haute)
19	Corrèze	44	Loire-Atlantique
2A	Corse-du-Sud	45	Loiret
2B	Haute-Corse	46	Lot
21	Côte-d'Or	47	Lot-et-Garonne
22	Côtes-d'Armor	48	Lozère
23	Creuse	49	Maine-et-Loire
24	Dordogne	50	Manche
25	Doubs	51	Marne

52	Marne (Haute)	74	Savoie (Haute)
53	Mayenne	75	Paris
54	Meurthe-et-Moselle	76	Seine-Maritime
55	Meuse	77	Seine-et-Marne
56	Morbihan	78	Yvelines
57	Moselle	79	Sèvres (Deux)
58	Nièvre	80	Somme
59	Nord	81	Tarn
60	Oise	82	Tarn-et-Garonne
61	Orne	83	Var
62	Pas-de-Calais	84	Vaucluse
63	Puy-de-Dôme	85	Vendée
64	Pyrénées-Atlantiques	86	Vienne
65	Pyrénées (Hautes)	87	Vienne (Haute)
66	Pyrénées-Orientales	88	Vosges
67	Rhin (Bas)	89	Yonne
68	Rhin (Haut)	90	Belfort (Territoire-de)
69	Rhône	91	Essonne
70	Saône (Haute)	92	Hauts-de-Seine
71	Saône-et-Loire	93	Seine-St-Denis
72	Sarthe	94	Val-de-Marne
73	Savoie	95	Val-d'Oise

14

French National Holidays

New Year's Day (*1 Jan*)

Easter Sunday and Monday

May Day (*1 May*)

Fête de la Libération (*8 May*)

Ascension Day

Whit Sunday and Monday

France's National Day (*14 July*)

The Assumption (*15 Aug*)

All Saints' Day (*1 Nov*)

Armistice Day (*11 Nov*)

Christmas Day (*25 Dec*)